THE LIFE OF PAUL

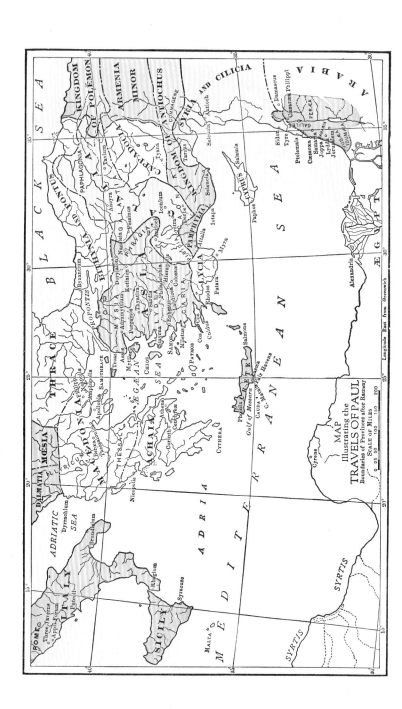

MAP
Illustrating the
TRAVELS OF PAUL
Boundaries of Provinces after Ramsay
SCALE OF MILES
0 25 50 100 150 200

THE LIFE OF PAUL

By

BENJAMIN WILLARD ROBINSON

THE UNIVERSITY OF CHICAGO PRESS

CHICAGO & LONDON

THE UNIVERSITY OF CHICAGO PRESS, CHICAGO & LONDON
The University of Toronto Press, Toronto 5, Canada

TO

Ernest DeWitt Burton

ὅτι με ἐπαίδευσας καλῶς, καὶ ἐκ τούτου ἐλπίζω ταχὺ
προκόσαι.—Soldier's Letter, Milligan, *Greek Papyri*, 36

PREFACE

The sources of knowledge of Paul's life are practically all contained in one volume, the New Testament. The source method of studying history can here be used with especial fitness. Modern scholarship has contributed much to a better understanding of the New Testament. The purpose of this handbook is to serve as a guide in so reading the ancient in the light of the modern that the student will be able to derive a clear and accurate conception of the apostle and his achievements.

He is advised first to read the New Testament references upon each stage of Paul's career, then to read the pages of this volume which supplement the references, and finally to study the references again with careful application of the textbook comments. He will do well at the same time to free his mind of rumors and notions concerning Paul and to think of him in his place among the leaders of history as a man of action with an international purpose to which he bent every energy of his powerful personality.

It is hoped that the instructor who uses the book will recognize the importance of regular assignments of "supplementary reading" with each chapter as well as the importance of having at hand a carefully selected reference library, such as is suggested in Appendix II. It is very desirable also that he find place for the discussion of certain subjects treated very briefly or not at all in the text, such subjects as are listed in Appendix III. Finally, he should use some method of conserving the student's reading and study, such as the outline life of Paul suggested in Appendix IV.

My indebtedness to the labors of others who have worked in this field will be apparent on every page. But I wish to express a sense of even greater obligation to those who have given so generously of their personal counsel and instruction, and particularly to the editors of this series, whose fellowship has been a constant and inspiring help.

BENJAMIN WILLARD ROBINSON

CHICAGO THEOLOGICAL SEMINARY

PREFACE TO THE REVISED EDITION

In response to many requests a chapter regarding Paul's religion has been added. Such a bare statement cannot hope to be more than an urgent invitation to the student to acquaint himself with some of the excellent books on this fascinating subject. Supplementary Readings and other bibliography have been revised. But in general the page-numbering and text of the first edition have been preserved as far as practicable.

Greetings to the many friends both near and far who have used this text or its Japanese translation. May the day be not far distant when the soul of humanity on the arduous road to Damascus shall find under the light of the spirit of Jesus, such a new life as came to the Apostle of old.

B. W. R.

TABLE OF CONTENTS

INTRODUCTORY NOTE

THE SOURCES

The two main sources of information concerning the life of Paul are the collection of his extant letters and the Book of Acts. Epistles are first-hand direct evidence. There are ten of these which fall within the period of the apostle's life which can be reconstructed with considerable certainty. The Pastoral Epistles constitute a study by themselves. Of the ten letters there are three which present certain problems of authorship, II Thessalonians, Colossians, and Ephesians. While there has been little general questioning of the genuineness of these, it is best to distinguish mentally between them and the others. Seven epistles are especially clear in their reflection of the circumstances and occasion of writing and in the information they incidentally afford concerning many other events in Paul's career. These seven are I Thessalonians, Galatians, I and II Corinthians, Romans, Philippians, and Philemon. These with the tentative inclusion of the other three mentioned above constitute our primary source.

The second source is the Book of Acts. Scholarship has much to say in favor of the general trustworthiness of that account. Luke, the "beloved physician," the author of the Gospel of Luke, wrote the Acts as a companion work to his Gospel. Both were probably written about the year 80. As in the Gospel Luke used Mark and other sources, so in Acts he undoubtedly employed earlier reports. In the first twelve or perhaps fifteen

chapters his main source was apparently a Jewish document written in Aramaic with many Old Testament
quotations.   In the latter half of the book, from 15:36
to the end, he was writing of events from which he was
himself not far removed.

In this latter half of the book there are four passages
written in the first person which are known as the "we"
sections.   They have been the subject of much study
and appear to be excerpts from a diary kept by a companion of Paul.   They describe portions of the second
and third journeys and the final voyage to Rome; these
passages are 16:10–17; 20:5–15; 21:1–18; 27:1—28:16.
Minute study of linguistic characteristics of these excerpts has shown that the author of the diary was the
same one who wrote the Book of Acts as a whole.   The
conclusion is that Luke himself was with Paul on these
occasions, and that later in writing the record of these
events he referred not only to his own memory but
probably also to an original notebook which he had kept.
Luke may have been with Paul at some other points also
where the narrative by use of the third person leaves the
author in the background.

In writing his book Luke had a large purpose in mind.
His was the first history of Christian missions.   Churches
in Ephesus and Corinth and other cities in the year 80
had little idea of how the gospel had reached them, of
their relation to other Christian groups throughout the
empire, or of what hardships Paul and others had suffered that the gospel might be brought to them.   Luke's
purpose was to give a panoramic view of the growth and
advance of Christianity from the little circle in Jerusalem to the climax in Paul's residence in Rome, the

capital of the world. He wished at the same time to inspire his readers with a faith and a courage which were worthy of those who had gone before.

In following out this large purpose he naturally omitted many things, greatly abbreviated others, and, in cases where his sources were fragmentary, filled in the gaps with the best information available. The speeches recorded illustrate his method. Addresses which would naturally occupy half an hour or an hour he has condensed into words which can be read in two or three minutes. Undoubtedly, too, there were occasions on which important and effective words were said of which he had no definite record. In such a case he would necessarily use his own best judgment in a statement of the gist of the address. In less than thirty chapters he covered more than thirty years of the expansion of early Christianity. Merely as history the book can rank with the work of Josephus and other great historians of antiquity. But it was written from quite a different point of view. Its purpose was not to recount the conquests of kings, to record battles and dates and treaties, but rather to portray the advance of a new force among the people, a force which bade fair to change the whole aspect of the life of the age.

In combining the facts reflected in Paul's letters with the information given in the Book of Acts our procedure will naturally be, first, to gather from the epistles all statements relative to the subject in hand, secondly, to add to these such details from the Book of Acts as fit readily and properly into the facts of the epistles. Where there appears any difference in narrative or point of view Paul's own words must be taken as our first guide, and Luke's words will be interpreted in the light of his remoter situation and of his particular purpose in writing. Thirdly, where Paul gives us no information and Luke is our only guide we shall follow him with no little confidence, always remembering that he may often be using an earlier written account and that in four sections at least he probably is using a diary kept at the time of the events themselves.

CHAPTER I

MEDITERRANEAN LIFE IN PAUL'S DAY

1. The Mediterranean World
2. The Jews of Palestine
3. The Jewish Dispersion
4. Political and Social Conditions in the Empire
5. Philosophies and Mystery-Religions
6. Emperor-Worship
7. "The Fulness of Time"

In connection with this chapter it is recommended that in place of a study of New Testament references an especially wide use be made of the supplementary readings given at the end of the chapter.

1. THE MEDITERRANEAN WORLD

Paul's life was spent in the lands bordering upon the Mediterranean Sea. His travels and his achievements were mainly along its irregular shores. The direct distance from Palestine at the eastern end to Spain, the western limit, is approximately 2,300 miles. The coast line, however, including the islands, measures over 10,000 miles. The orange, the fig, and the olive tree, found throughout its length, indicate the mildness and general uniformity of the climate.

The first decisive step toward unification of this world of the Mediterranean was taken by Alexander the Great. He was the pioneer in successfully mingling the western and eastern civilizations. Had it not been for his interweaving of Greeks and Semites it would have been quite impossible for any enterprise to spread from Palestine to the west with such rapidity as characterized the Christian missionary accomplishments of the first century.

In fact Christianity's line of march westward was strikingly close to Alexander's route eastward. Alexander "came over" from Macedonia to Asia. Proceeding through Mysia he crossed the Taurus Mountains at the Cilician Gates and fought his most decisive battle near Antioch (Issus, 333 B.C.). He spent a long while at Tyre and Gaza. He paid great respect to the Temple at Jerusalem. Christianity in its march in the opposite direction advanced from Jerusalem to Gaza, to Tyre, all along the coast. At Antioch the disciples were first called Christians. From Antioch as a center Paul started out upon his great European trip, crossing the mountains at the Cilician Gates, passing by Mysia through Asia, and came over into Macedonia. Alexander had paved the road along which Paul advanced in his gospel campaign westward.

The composite civilization which resulted from Alexander's conquests was not Greek in the strict sense of the word. The new culture was modified by contact with many different nationalities. But since it arose in direct connection with the extension of Greek ideas and customs, and of a universalized form of the Greek language, it has been called the Hellenistic civilization. In this Hellenistic world the Jews both of Palestine and of the Dispersion constituted an important factor.

2. THE JEWS OF PALESTINE

The eastward march of the Greek culture had a far-reaching influence on the history and ideas of the Jews.

Palestine was the only land route for communication between Syria and Egypt, between Asia and Africa. In the international intercourse which Alexander aroused, the Jews, who had always considered themselves a people set apart and holy, found themselves as never before in the channel of commerce and military campaign. Hellenistic culture was gradually, irresistibly permeating the Holy Land. Greek cities were springing up which later combined themselves in the very midst of Judaism into the league called the Decapolis.

During the last two centuries before Christ the Jews were almost continually engaged in long struggles against encroaching Hellenism. So long as they were fighting for religious liberty and spiritual ideals they were repeatedly successful, even against great odds. They were able to avenge themselves when a Syrian king desecrated the Temple. They were able to win the privilege of minting their own imageless coins. They again and again established their right to worship Jehovah in their own way. Often political power and even considerable military conquest seemed just within their reach. But, like Tantalus, they never quite succeeded in grasping and holding in any satisfying way the object of their desire. It was with their life-blood that they paid the price of such territorial and imperial aspirations. Yet as armies marched back and forth, as Greek cities sprang up in their midst, as the Greek language and Roman power became facts of their daily life, they felt more than ever that as God's chosen people they had been chosen for some sort of a mission among the nations of the world. This world-mission they began to realize must be a religious, not a political, one.

They turned their attention increasingly to the careful study and explanation of their scriptures and to the making of converts. Their ideal was first to perfect their system of worship and secondly to make Jerusalem the Mecca of the world. They became less military, more religious, less nationalistic, more evangelistic. In their deeper searching after God's will the Jewish leaders thought to find it in a more exact keeping of the letter of the law. The result was the elaborate ceremonial system of the Pharisees. Though not always observed with inner sincerity of heart, it was intended as an expression of increased loyalty to their God in the face of the great new civilization which was approaching.

In all their experiences was the hope and confidence that God would some day consummate in divine fashion all their ideals. Oppression and wickedness would be destroyed. The Jews would be freed and exalted. Usually, but not universally, they expected that the consummation would be brought about by a mighty leader whom Jehovah would "anoint" for the task.

The "Messiah," i.e., the "anointed one," was pictured in many ways. Popularly he was conceived as a heavenly being whom God would send down to earth with miraculous power to establish social justice. In that new day each Jew would be able to sit under his own vine and fig tree, and there would be none to make afraid. Among religious leaders and among thoughtful Jews generally there was considerable emphasis upon uprightness of conduct as the principal condition of entrance into that new kingdom. And the Messiah was pictured as a great prophet whom Jehovah would endow with wisdom and with the spirit. He would teach all men Jehovah's greatness and goodness.   Only the utterly godless would be rejected.   Upon all who would accept it the spirit would be poured out from on high.   Men would be endowed with a capacity and a desire for purity and brotherhood.

Many of these tendencies of late Judaism were found in a Christianized form in the early church.   The intense devotion to God's will accompanied by a turning away from present political and economic problems, the increased acquaintance with other nations, the proselyting activity, the emphasis upon righteousness rather than literal Abrahamic descent as the basis of acceptability before God, the expectation of a messianic kingdom soon to appear—all these it is essential to keep in mind in any study of early Christianity in relation to contemporary Jewish thought.

3. THE JEWISH DISPERSION

During the third century B.C., when Egypt controlled Palestine, Jews migrated in large numbers to Alexandria, so named after Alexander the Great.   There they formed a considerable colony in the city, adopted the Greek language, and translated the Old Testament into Greek.   In the second century B.C., when Syrian power became dominant in Palestine, the Jews migrated northward and settled in large numbers around Antioch. They went farther into Cilicia, following the line of march of Alexander over into the cities of Asia Minor, Macedonia, and Greece.   After Pompey and the Roman armies conquered Palestine in the first century B.C. the dispersion of the Jews gradually reached to the ends of the Roman Empire.

As a result of this dispersion Paul found his fellow-countrymen in almost every city he wished to visit. There are definite traces of a hundred and fifty such Jewish communities. It would be hard to overestimate the importance of these little groups throughout the empire as a series of advanced posts from which the gospel could be preached.

The simplicity and modesty of the little Jewish synagogue would be very striking to one who walked along the streets of an ancient city. The fact that there was no altar would impress him at once. The worshiper who was seeking communion with the eternal God was becoming skeptical about bowing down to beautifully carved images and statues. Each Sabbath the Jews assembled to pray to the unseen God and to listen to his revelation as contained in the Prophets. A desk for reading and benches for sitting would be almost the only furniture in the room. The candlestick and a few lamps kept burning would be an effective symbol of the Light of God burning in the human soul. Perhaps there would be a finely wrought box in which the records of the Holy Scriptures were kept. But in general the simplicity and spirituality of the atmosphere would be its greatest appeal.

These synagogues of the Dispersion kept in close touch with the mother-community at Jerusalem. Every spring at Passover time delegates were sent to the celebrations. The list in the second chapter of Acts reaches from Mesopotamia in the east to Rome in the west. Every Jew hoped to see the Temple once in his life, and if possible frequently. Each synagogue was expected to contribute to the support of the elaborate worship at

Jerusalem. In the spread of the Christian gospel this unity of the Dispersion was of great importance. Almost as serum injected into the blood is carried to all parts of the body, so Christianity was carried out along the great arteries already established into the remotest parts of the empire.

A further significant fact was the liberalizing influence of living in the large cities of the empire. The Hebrew religion was to a large extent adapted to the new environment. The ceremonial of the Jewish law which could not be observed without great inconvenience was reduced to a minimum. Greater emphasis was placed upon ethical and spiritual requirements. The Greek translation of the Hebrew Scriptures was used. This Greek version, which does not agree in all particulars with the Hebrew, was the Bible of Paul's churches and gentile Christianity in general. In the vigorous proselyting activity many concessions to gentile points of view were made. Large use of allegory in interpreting the Scripture helped to bridge the way to the principles of Greek philosophy. Thus while in Jerusalem the Jews were becoming ceremonially legalistic to an extreme, in the Roman world at large the religion of the Jews was interpreting itself in terms which appealed to the nations of the empire.

There is one further feature of the life of the Dispersion which is of paramount importance for the understanding of Paul's success. Throughout the empire were many men who felt that the exalted Jewish conception of God was the true one, but who were unwilling to go to the ceremonial extent of having themselves circumcised and in other ways conforming to Jewish requirements.

Cornelius the centurion is described in Acts 10:2 as a devout man and one who feared God with all his house, gave much alms to the people, and prayed to God always. Yet this man was considered technically unclean by Peter until after his vision. This class of men, mentioned frequently in the Book of Acts among the Dispersion, are called those "that fear God." They constituted a considerable section in the attendance upon every synagogue of the Dispersion. They were not considered Jews. They were excluded from Jewish privileges and to a certain extent regarded as "unclean" by the Jews merely because they revolted at certain ceremonial requirements. To these men the word that the Mosaic law had been superseded would come with peculiar power and force. Trained in prophetic ideals, they were ready and eager for just such a message as Paul brought.

4. POLITICAL AND SOCIAL CONDITIONS IN THE EMPIRE

From the Battle of Actium in 31 B.C. to the end of his long reign in 14 A.D. the emperor Augustus applied himself to the unification of the civilized world. He was fundamentally devoted to the cause of peace and order and was possessed of a strong will to carry out his purpose. He ushered in the most prosperous period of antiquity. Tiberius, who followed Augustus, also had a long and outwardly peaceful reign (14 to 37). Both he and Claudius (41 to 54), who came to the throne after the short intervening reign of Caligula (37 to 41), were interested in building up the life of the provinces and in uniting the empire. Toleration and harmony were everywhere encouraged and, if necessary, enforced.

The various nationalities came to know each other's customs and creeds. Never had the world known itself so well. There was one language which could be used almost everywhere. Egyptians, Judeans, Syrians, Cilicians, Galatians, Macedonians, and Romans could speak and understand Greek. The New Testament was written in this language, although most of its writers were Jews. Travel became easy because of the development of road systems and lines of sailing vessels. It became safe because travelers, especially any who had attained Roman citizenship, were rigorously protected wherever they went. The right of appeal to the emperor insured against local persecution.

That the life of Paul's day was more than eighteen centuries behind us in time, that its scenes were in lands thousands of miles removed from America, that it was without the multitude of conveniences that modern invention has produced, might make in our minds the impression that the life itself must be widely different from our own. But the glimpses into that life which we have in recent years gained through the discovery of papyrus fragments that have lain for centuries in the sands of Egypt have revealed a lively activity which is by no means strange or distant. As we read these scraps of personal correspondence, Paul's letters take on new life and freshness.

The travel of the time is reflected in many papyrus notes. One is a letter written home by a tourist who has been "doing" the Nile and studying the ancient Egyptian temples that he may, to use his own expression, "learn about the works made by men's hands" (cf. Acts 17:24). Incidentally he confesses to scratching names on the walls of the sanctuaries "for perpetual remembrance." Another is a letter of recommendation such as Paul insisted he did not need to the Corinthians. Another is a request from an Athenian to the folks at home to send an overcoat. He has been caught in a spell of cold weather such as perhaps caused Paul to send for that cloak he left at Troas with Carpus (Milligan, *Greek Pap.* No. 26; Goodspeed, No. 4; Deissmann, *Light from the East*, No. 1).

New glimpses into family life and relationships are particularly numerous. One man writes another requesting the loan of dishes and many other things for a house party. He asks incidentally for some bronze cymbals. When Paul told the Corinthians that a Christian without love is like "a clanging cymbal," he was using no uncertain or unfamiliar illustration (*Hibeh Pap.*, No. 54). The same letter speaks of a runaway slave and hopes for his speedy arrest. Perhaps that slave did not receive as kindly treatment as Paul probably secured for the runaway Onesimus. The position of slaves, however, improved in Paul's day. Claudius was the first to make the killing of a slave a capital offense.

Another letter reflects a death scene in the home. Philo and his wife have lost their son. The mother is in great grief. Her friend Irene writes her a letter meant to be one of consolation: "I wept over the death of your son," she writes, "as much as I did when my own child Didymas passed away." Notice the pathos of her hopelessness as she closes her letter with these words: "Against such things one can do nothing." To such families Paul came with his cheering words, as he did at Thessalonica: "Sorrow not even as the rest who have no hope" (Milligan, *Greek Pap.*, No. 38).

Here is a letter which a prodigal son has written home on a frayed sheet of papyrus. He has heard from his friend Postumus that his mother had gone to the metropolis to look for him. If he had only known, he would have dared to go there to meet her, but he did not have the courage to go home to his own village. "I want you to know," he writes, "that I had no idea you would go to the metropolis. And that is the reason I did not come. And I was ashamed to come to Caranis [his home] because I go about in rags. I write to you that I am naked. I beseech you, mother, be reconciled to me. I know what I have brought upon myself. I have been chastened every day. I know that I have sinned—I beseech thee . . . ." The rest of the letter is so worn and torn that we cannot read it. It may be that the mother's tears aided in making it illegible (Milligan, *Greek Pap.*, No. 37).

Of the life of soldiers there are many reflections in the letters which they wrote home. One young recruit who has just completed the journey, probably his first sea voyage, from his home in Egypt to the training camp in Italy, writes of his dire "danger at sea," is thankful for his "rescue," sends his "picture" (probably taken in his new uniform), hopes for a "promotion" in the near future, and begs for news from home. He uses the margin lengthwise for greetings to his friends (Milligan, *Greek Pap.*, No. 36).

Here is another in the latest volume of *Oxyrhynchus Papyri* (Vol. XII, No. 1481). It is from one of the boys "in camp." He is writing to his distracted mother, who has heard by some roundabout way of his being laid up. "Don't be distressed. I was greatly distressed to hear that you had heard; for I was not seriously disabled. And I blame the man who told you." Though he was not a Christian, but a worshiper of Isis, he shows his Christian solicitude as he thinks of the shortage at home by writing in his letter and repeating again in the margin: "Don't trouble to be sending us anything."

Paul was one of many travelers who went from country to country. On his journeys he wrote letters as others did. Although he employed his letters as a means of instruction, nevertheless there are constant points of contact in phrase and illustration with the life of the time. He talked about temples not "made with hands." He spoke of bondage and slavery and redemption. He used the same word as the prodigal son when he spoke of being "reconciled" to God. In a world familiar with military affairs, he begged men to put on his new kind of breastplate and helmet. He entered into almost every phase of the life of the great cities and expressed himself in the simple, direct language of the people to whom he came.

5. PHILOSOPHIES AND MYSTERY-RELIGIONS

The development and spread of philosophy, especially since the days of Alexander, had had an important and far-reaching influence on the religious thinking of multitudes of people throughout the Roman Empire. Plato and after him the Stoics had given wide currency to the belief in one supreme God and the possibility of life after death. The Epicureans had helped to make the popular polytheism ridiculous. Cynics and Stoics both gave much attention to the ethical aspects of every-day life. Nor were these leadings of the philosophers the possession of the learned only; they were spread abroad by conversational tracts, called *diatribé*. Rarely perhaps has philosophy more effectively reached and influenced the masses.

The result of this process was threefold: (1) The popular polytheism, with its belief in a multitude of gods greater and lesser, lost its hold upon men. Even those who like the Epicureans and others used the old phrases did not believe in the ideas for which they once stood. (2) In its place a philosophic monotheism was taught by the philosophers and widely accepted. (3) The decay of the old polytheism, the deepening of ethical thought, and the belief in the possibility of a future life all tended to create a hunger for a religion of the individual which could elevate life, give fellowship with God, and assure one of immortality. Into a world thus hungry the so-called mystery-religions came with their answers to all these demands.

The more popular of these were the Eleusinian Mysteries of Greece, the Mysteries of Mithra from Persia, the Mysteries of Isis from Egypt, and the Cybele-Attis Mysteries from Asia Minor. All these religions were seeking an answer to the greatest needs of life and death. They aimed to help a man to overcome himself, his fears, his lower nature, his insidious, destructive sins. They put him in touch with the unseen, the eternal, the abiding, the exalting, the spiritual. Many a man who had been initiated into one of these sacred cults became a better man. In most cases a candidate for admission after praying and fasting had to wash himself thoroughly as a token that he would thereafter keep himself not only physically pure but mentally and spiritually as well. Then he would take certain oaths. In the Eleusinian Mysteries he must promise to be "pure of hand" and "pure of soul." He must feel that the deity may speak to him and through him, be reconciled to him, deliver him from sin. In this partnership with deity was to be his assurance of immortality.

In the famous description of the initiation of Lucius into the Mysteries of Isis at Cenchreae (Apuleius, *Metam.* xi. 18–25), the symbolic washings are described and ten days of secluded meditation. Then Lucius was conducted through a series of scenes in the temple depicting the experience of death, the abode of the blessed after death, and the glory of standing in the presence of the gods. The net effect of the whole initiation was to create an indelible impression of the badness of evil and the eternal nobility of goodness, to make the initiate forget his petty pains or pleasures and to live mindful of the truth, proved by philosophy, that his soul had an eternal destiny.

But along with the good and the inspiring features of these religions were many useless and superstitious and even pernicious practices. Those "mysteries" which appealed to the senses and the passions naturally tended to be more popular. In many cases a man who worked himself into a frenzy by dancing or drinking or mere play upon his emotions was considered to be nearer the deity than a man in his right mind.

It was into a world already seeking to satisfy its deep longing with philosophy or with the mystery-religions of the East that Paul came with his message, kindred in many respects with theirs, for he too taught the doctrine of the one God living and true, purity of life, and life after death achieved through fellowship with the divine spirit, yet different also, especially in the far greater simplicity of his doctrine and of the fewer ceremonies that were associated with it.   For Paul dared to hope that a purely spiritual religion would triumph, because men eventually choose the highest and the best.   It was this confidence that gave him courage to preach throughout the Roman Empire his gospel of faith in a crucified Christ, the revelation of the all-loving Father, and of fellowship with him.

6. EMPEROR-WORSHIP

The attempt of Rome to institute a religion of the empire was part of the government's policy of unification. The world was one politically.   The nations were uniting upon one language.   Why should not the peoples share in a common religion?   Nor was exaltation of the supreme ruler as an object of worship a new idea in the world.   Both in Egypt and in Babylon departed rulers were from early days deified and pictured as enjoying fellowship with the gods.   The transition from calling a dead ruler a god to calling his living son divine was an easy one in the Orient.   The word "divine" came to be applied regularly to rulers of Egypt during their lifetime. With the approbation of Rome this general attitude spread gradually westward.

If Alexander the Great had been worshiped along with the gods after his death, if even in Athens Aristotle had had an altar erected to Plato, why should not the great Pompey be called "divine," as the proclamation in Athens stated? And finally in Rome why should anyone be shocked to hear the decree of the Senate in 42 B.C. that Julius Caesar should be called "Julius, the divine one"? During the first century A.D., especially in the provinces at a distance from Rome, there was a steadily increasing custom of speaking of the living emperor as divine and of offering incense to him. It had little to do with the longing and groping for that Spiritual Being which their philosophy told them existed, but whom they were unable to find in any real and satisfying way.

From the viewpoint of the worshiper the emperor cult was akin to the old Greek hero-worship. Those who like Hercules had done great deeds or had rendered great service to their country were loaded with honors, were regarded as demigods, and were supposed to have gone at their death to the realms above. Augustus did much for the people. The cessation of the constant civil war and the better organization of the provinces won for him intense gratitude everywhere. Hope revived that now perhaps at length the long years of suffering and oppression were at an end. Virgil sung that the cycle of ages had completed its circuit and the golden era was about to begin again. Justice was about to return and fear to be banished from the earth. Augustus was often called the saver, or savior, of the whole earth. He was spoken of as the son of a god and himself divine. The fact that Augustus himself publicly declined these epithets did not detract from popular enthusiasm.

As years rolled on and still the perfect commonwealth was not realized, as oppression and injustice continued, people looked for their benefactor in the person of other later emperors. Claudius (41–54 A.D.), who was emperor during much of Paul's missionary activity, was a good ruler. He was another who was called savior of the world. When Paul talked of a savior and of salvation he was using terms which were very real to the peoples of the empire. Disappointed hopes revived and longings for a freer and larger life were awakened.

7. "THE FULNESS OF TIME"

The general situation may be briefly stated under three heads: (1) the Jews of Palestine, (2) the Dispersion, (3) the Graeco-Roman world in general.

1. Politically, the Jews of Palestine had been through severe experiences in the last centuries before Christ. Many Jews had begun to realize that God's "chosen" people were not chosen to be military leaders. When they had fought for religious liberty they had again and again been successful, but when they had pushed on toward political conquest they had not often been prosperous. They were turning their efforts toward a more perfect interpretation of their religion and to the making of converts. Socially, the Jews had become acquainted with other peoples. After the time of Alexander the Great, Greek culture and Greek ideas had irresistibly penetrated Palestine. The holy and separate people was becoming increasingly a highway of the nations. Religiously, the messianic hope had been deepened and likewise broadened. Emphasis on the ethical and spiritual was crowding out narrow nationalistic ideas. The expected Kingdom took on an international aspect to a greater extent than ever before.

2. Between Palestinian Judaism and the Western World there had developed a mediating agency, the Jewish Dispersion. It was a migration of Jews from Palestine to avoid war and persecution or to acquire money and position. They had settled in colonies in every important center of the empire. They were not only everywhere upholding the Jewish ideals of mono- theism and ethical purity, but were steadily making converts to their faith. Socially, the various groups maintained close relationship with the mother-country and with each other. This unity made the Dispersion an effective instrument for quickly spreading throughout the world the news of any new prophet or Messiah who might appear. Religiously, these Jews of the Disper- sion were not so narrow in their point of view as the leaders at Jerusalem. They naturally had to omit temple sacrifices and many ceremonial observances. They came into contact with the peoples of the world, with the large ideas of Greek philosophy, and with the practical ways of Roman leadership.

Of particular significance was that outer circle of gentile converts who refused to believe in the necessity of circumcision and of ceremonial in general, but who nevertheless were convinced that the Jews were right in declaring that there was but one God who guided all things and who demanded righteousness of his followers. These men and women, not called Jews nor even prose- lytes, but simply the "devout" ones or the ones who "fear God," were the keystone in the arch of the bridge which led from Jerusalem to the peoples of the world.

3. In the Graeco-Roman world at large many differ- ent tendencies were to have an influence on the career of

Paul. Politically, the Roman government had ushered
in an era of peace. War had practically ceased. The
time of Augustus was a sort of Golden Age. The policy
of universal toleration of all religions and creeds gave
Christianity a chance to make its appeal. The whole
Mediterranean world had come under this one government. Socially, the result of the political unity was a
mingling of peoples such as can be paralleled only in
America in modern times. So thorough was this intercourse that one language was everywhere spoken and
understood. In addition to the unity of language there
was the unusual development of commerce. Navigation
lines and well-paved roads connected all important points
of the empire. Travel had never been so easy nor so
safe as in the first century. Religiously, the peoples had
awakened. Philosophical monotheism had started over
the empire a wave of atheism which had largely broken
the charm of the religions of Greece and Rome. There
was a real desire to find God. Educated men were turning to the great spiritual doctrines of Stoicism; others
were looking to the East and finding inadequate satis-
faction in the mystery-religions.

The tendency toward monotheism and the consequent discrediting of polytheism, the various attempts
by the people to commune with God in the mystery-
religions, the intensity with which the people were
looking for a new age and an empire of justice and
brotherhood and happiness in place of oppression and
domination and misery, show that the messianic hope
was not confined to the Jews. There was a flood
of waiting expectation which we may justly call
the messianic hope of the world. an international,

universal longing for the day when men "shall live
the life of gods."

> The base degenerate iron offspring ends,
> A golden progeny from heaven descends.
> The jarring nations he in peace shall bind
> And with paternal virtues rule mankind.
>
> —Virgil, *Fourth Eclogue.*

SUPPLEMENTARY READING

1. Foakes-Jackson, *Saint Paul*, pp. 25–48.
2. Foakes-Jackson and Lake, *Beginnings of Christianity*, I, 218–62.
3. Breasted, *Ancient Times*, pp. 425–83.
4. Goodspeed, *History of the Ancient World*, pp. 357–96.
5. Kent, *Work and Teachings of the Apostles*, pp. 9–20.
6. Dill, *Roman Society*, pp. 289–383.
7. Case, *Evolution of Early Christianity*, pp. 48–77, 284–330.
8. Angus, *Environment of Early Christianity*, pp. 68–139.
9. Kennedy, *St. Paul and the Mystery-Religions*, pp. 68–114.
10. Deissmann, *St. Paul*, pp. 29–54.
11. McGiffert, *A History of Christianity in the Apostolic Age*, pp. 151–60.
12. Milligan, *Greek Papyri*, pp. xix–xxxii, Nos. 8, 26, 36, 37, 38.

CHAPTER II

PAUL'S YOUTH

1. Boyhood at Tarsus
   Acts 21:39; 22:3, 27, 28; 23:6; Phil. 3:5; I Sam.
   9:1, 2; Acts 18:3
2. Training at Jerusalem
   Acts 22:3; 23:16; 26:4; 5:34; Gal. 1:14
3. Jewish Law as a Schoolmaster
   Acts 26:5; Phil. 3:5; Gal. 3:23–25
4. Paul's Personal Traits
   (1) Phil. 3:5 *vs.* Acts 22:28
   (2) Acts 22:3; I Cor. 2:6 *vs.* I Cor. 4:12; Acts 20:34, 35
   (3) Gal. 1:17; I Cor. 9:27; II Cor. 12:4 *vs.* I Cor. 9:22;
       II Cor. 13:1–3
   (4) Gal. 4:13; II Cor. 12:7 *vs.* II Cor. 11:23–27.
       I Cor. 9:24, 25 *vs.* Gal. 2:20; 5:16
   (5) Phil. 4:7 *vs.* Eph. 6:11, 13–17; I Thess. 5:8; II Tim.
       4:7
   (6) I Cor. 2:3; 15:9 *vs.* II Cor. 11:5; 12:11

1. BOYHOOD AT TARSUS

Paul was "a citizen of no mean city." Tarsus, on
the river Cydnus in the fertile Cilician plain about twelve
miles from the sea, was an important center with an
illustrious history. Before the conquests of Alexander
it had been an oriental town. Then a university was
founded. The Romans recognized the prominence of
the place and favored it. Cicero lived here while governor of Cilicia (51–50 B.C.). It was here that Anthony
in 38 B.C. summoned Cleopatra to appear before him.

Here she voyaged up the river with her gaily dressed rowers and silvered oars, conquering Anthony by her beauty and her charm. Here lived Athenodorus, who taught the emperor Augustus. In 22 B.C. Augustus not only confirmed the freedom of the city, but gave it the title of "metropolis" and the right to issue its own coins with that title upon them.

The geographer Strabo, who lived from 54 B.C. to 24 A.D., says that Tarsus ranked above Athens and Alexandria as a center of the study of philosophy. Apollonius studied here in the first century, and later Theodore of Mopsuestia, and Chrysostom. Close by Tarsus, in Soli, was the home of Aratus the poet (270 B.C.), whom Paul quoted in his Athenian address.

Located midway between the East and the West, Tarsus was a transition point for travel both on land and on sea. Because of its nearness to the famous Cilician Gates (3,600 feet) it was a natural stopping-place for the overland commerce and culture which flowed in both directions through the Taurus Mountains. And along the banks of the river the ships came in from both East and West and docked. There sailors from Syria and sailors from Greece would meet, and there the Jewish scholar disembarking from one boat would see the Roman scholar landing from another. Both would walk up the same street toward the university.

It is true that Tarsus was very different from Nazareth, where Jesus spent his boyhood. Nazareth was rural, closer to nature. Tarsus was an industrial center, more cosmopolitan. Jesus had much to say about animals and natural scenery. Paul drew his illustrations largely from city life.

Yet it is noteworthy that the home of Jesus and the home of Paul had certain characteristics in common. In Nazareth Jesus could in a few minutes walk from his home to a ridge where he could view the snows of Hermon, 10,000 feet high. In like manner Paul saw, near by, the snows of the Taurus Range. Who shall say that Paul did not now and then climb these lofty mountains and thereby develop not only an upward look but a certain physical persistence which was his peculiar heritage?

From his home in Nazareth Jesus could look out upon the plain of Esdraelon and see the caravans of the nations passing on their way from Damascus to Egypt. In like manner Paul in his youth must often have spent mornings upon the wharves looking with curiosity upon the ships that came in. He would be fascinated; he would dream such dreams as Sir Walter Raleigh dreamed while haunting the wharves of old Portsmouth. Visions of far countries, of strange cities, of great deeds, must have come to the keen eyes and roaming thoughts of the Jewish boy.

Again, not very far from Nazareth the boy Jesus could catch a glimpse of the Mediterranean at two little V-shaped openings in the hills. The sea would speak to him of the bigness of the world. Tarsus, too, is but a few miles from the coast. The boy Paul could in intervals of work or study visit the hillside and look out over the blue waters with their many sails.

The effect upon the boys was to develop an exalted and large view of human existence. Both Jesus and Paul lived very close to life. Both understood men.

Yet in their leadership both looked above and beyond. They knew the lowest and the highest in life, the daily task and the distant goal.

As Paul grew to self-consciousness he would feel a triple pride which would distinguish him from his playmates and convince him in his earliest years that he was destined for no ordinary career. First of all he would be proud of his birthplace. Every year as the holidays rolled round which celebrated the remarkable events in the city's history he would become more and more familiar with the exploits of the noted men who had lived and labored there.

A second and larger element in his pride would be his distinguished Jewish lineage. There would be few if any others in Tarsus who could claim descent from the favored Benjamin. Saul was the name of the first monarch and greatest soldier of Israel, whose description would be among the first lessons in the Scriptures. As a growing boy Paul would strive zealously to imitate his royal ancestor whose name he bore and to become "from his shoulders and upward higher than any of the people." Surely he later attained that ideal in a nobler than the physical sense.

The third and most distinguishing element in his pride would be his father's Roman citizenship. From his earliest years he would be as proud of his Roman name Paul as of his Jewish name Saul. It is extremely unlikely that there was another family in Tarsus of the tribe of Benjamin which enjoyed the honor of Roman citizenship. Throughout his life we may believe he maintained this triple pride, in Tarsus, in the tribe of Benjamin, in Roman birth.

Paul probably remained in Tarsus until he was about fifteen years of age. His chief schooling was naturally at the Jewish synagogue school. The language of instruction was Greek, and the Greek version of the Scriptures was his Bible. But he learned to read the Old Testament in Hebrew. His first lessons would perhaps consist in memorizing sections of the Law and the Prophets both in Greek and in Hebrew. Before leaving Tarsus he would probably be able to read intelligently many parts of the Hebrew Scriptures and be familiar with sections of interpretations of famous Jewish rabbis.

Either during these years or later he learned the trade of tent-making. There is no reason to suppose that his father was especially poor. Every Jewish boy was taught a trade. If he was ambitious to become a teacher, it was especially important to have some way of earning a living, for teachers were paid even less in that day than now. While the exact nature of his trade of "tent-making" is not entirely clear, we are fairly safe in concluding that he learned to weave the coarse tent-cloth, to throw the shuttle and shift the threads for the return throw, as is so common in the Orient today.

2. TRAINING AT JERUSALEM

Paul was a traveler. It was in his blood and in the air he breathed. From his earliest days he had heard stories of the home of the tribe of Benjamin and of the magnificence of the Jewish temple. In Acts 22:3 the words "brought up in this city" indicate that Paul went to Jerusalem while still very young. He probably had relatives in Jerusalem with whom he could stay (cf. Acts 23:16). At the age of fifteen or sixteen, with his baggage packed in leather bags, he embarked at Tarsus upon one of the big ships bound for the coast of Palestine.

He would sail down the Cydnus out into the wide waters and, after a night of much anticipation and little sleep, would watch the shores of Syria as his ship moved southward. Majestic Lebanon and Hermon would pass by. Bold Mount Carmel, thrusting itself forward into the sea, would speak of Elijah and the early warriors of God. The mountains of Judea would be to him reminders of Amos, of Isaiah, of Jeremiah, of the other prophets who formed and fostered the faith of Israel.

He would land at Caesarea, which, long after the days of Jonah, had superseded Joppa as the port of Jerusalem. He would admire the Roman castle built out into the water, little dreaming that he was later to spend two years as a prisoner there. The journey up to Jerusalem could be easily made in two days on horseback. The second morning would be especially exhilarating, as the road ascended to magnificent views of the plain and the sea, reaching at Jerusalem a height of 2,600 feet.

The Temple with its central sanctuary and its outlying buildings was one of the most elaborate and costly places of worship in the Roman Empire. What the palace of the emperor was to Rome, what the Acropolis with its unparalleled Parthenon was to Greece, such was the Temple to Jerusalem and to the Dispersion throughout the empire. Herod the Great had lavished his extravagance upon it. Forty years it had been building, and still the beautifying and the adding of further buildings continued. The youthful Paul would enter the outer court with a certain sense of ownership. In the "Court of the Gentiles" he would carefully read that ominous inscription decreeing death to any Gentile who passed beyond. Then with some awe and with some pride in his Jewish birth he would enter the inner court. Either there or outside he might on his first day meet his instructor, Gamaliel.

Gamaliel was a man well fitted to develop Paul's mind and spirit. There were two schools of instruction competing with each other for first place in Jerusalem. From our modern point of view both were narrow and provincial. But one put more emphasis upon the petty details of the law, while the other was capable of larger interpretation. When a Gentile came to Shammai and promised to be his pupil, if he would summarize the whole law while standing on one foot, Shammai sent him off in disgust. When Hillel was confronted with the same proposition his answer was ready, "Do not do to your neighbor anything which you would not like to have him do to you."

Gamaliel, who was probably the grandson of Hillel, went so far as to make references to Greek works in his interpretations. His broadmindedness is reflected in an interesting scene in the book of Acts $(5:34)$. Gamaliel, "a doctor of the law, had in honor of all the people," a Pharisee, rose up in the council when the Jewish leaders were about to deal violently with the Christian apostles. "Refrain from these men and let them alone," he advised, "for if this work be of men it will be overthrown: but if it is of God ye will not be able to overthrow them." Yet Gamaliel dealt sharply with those who opposed him. Many tales are told to illustrate the fact that Gamaliel could never be vanquished in any argument nor changed in his opinion.

Paul's Roman citizenship and his boyhood in Tarsus furnished a favorable basis for a broad outlook upon the world. By nature he was resolute and determined. In Gamaliel he found an instructor who combined a tendency to broadmindedness with an unflinching courage of conviction, traits which were later to play no small part in Paul's career.

3. JEWISH LAW AS A SCHOOLMASTER

In Galatians Paul says that the law is a tutor to bring us to Christ and adds: "Now that faith has come we are no longer under a tutor." Paul's life as a Jew was not wholly lost time. It had its definite part in bringing him to Christ. Much he had to unlearn, but much also he retained as part of his Christian effectiveness. His zeal as a Pharisee of the "straightest sect" was not an evil to be overcome but a force which was to be turned into a new channel for the healing of the nations.

Concerning Paul's life in Jerusalem our information is very meager. How long did he continue his studies under Gamaliel? Was he in Jerusalem in the Temple when Jesus at twelve years of age was found entertaining the rabbis? Was he in the city at all during Jesus' ministry? How old was Paul when Jesus was crucified? One very small coincidence is certain. If Jesus went every year with his parents (Luke 2:41) to Jerusalem from twelve years of age to thirty, the two boys must have been in Jerusalem together more than once.

That Paul never met Jesus in the flesh seems certain. When his enemies at Corinth discredited his apostleship on the ground that he had never seen Jesus, his answer was a reference to the appearance of the risen Christ (I Cor. 9:1; 15:8; cf. II Cor. 11:22 ff.). Nor could he have been in Jerusalem at all during the great scenes of Jesus' ministry there, for he makes no claim to have direct external knowledge of those events.

During the ministry of Jesus, Paul was probably at home again in Tarsus. After completing a course of several years under Gamaliel at Jerusalem he would still have little familiarity with Greek literature and philosophy. In view of the prominence of the university at Tarsus it is unlikely that Paul would take no advantage of his opportunity there. While he might not as a strict Jew pursue as thorough a course of study as he had probably done at Jerusalem, he would at least gain a general knowledge of Greek thought and history.

It is not impossible that Paul made some trips into other districts and provinces as a part of his education. The men of Tarsus were known as travelers, and later at least Paul traveled extensively. As a persecutor of Christians Paul extended his activities "even unto foreign cities" (Acts 26:11). As a Christian he planned his journeys far ahead of him. When he had gone as far as Ephesus he planned to go to Rome (Acts 19:21). When he had reached Corinth he wrote of journeying to Spain (Rom. 15:24). Whether in these early years his travels were extensive is impossible to say. Perhaps he went as far as the coast cities of Asia Minor, Ephesus and Smyrna and Troas.

After some years at Tarsus he returned to Jerusalem, probably to realize a dream of becoming a rabbi. He made advances in Jewish learning and scholarship beyond many of his own age (Gal. 1:14). One passage in Acts indicates that he became a member of the ruling council of Jerusalem, the Sanhedrin. This is the implication of the statement in Acts 26:10 that he gave his vote for the death penalty against followers of Jesus. He could not, however, expect to attain the title of rabbi until he was forty years of age. Meanwhile he lived as a Pharisee, a Hebrew of the Hebrews, an adept in all the rabbinical discussions between the school of Shammai and the school of Hillel.

There are many traces in Paul's Christian writings of his Jewish Pharisaic training. The argument of Gal. 3:16 based upon the difference between the singular and the plural of the word "seed" shows the kind of exegetical method which Paul learned. A similar instance is the allegory of Sarah and Hagar in the same letter. A particularly interesting instance is Paul's use of the Mosaic law: "Thou shalt not muzzle the ox when he treadeth out the corn." Asking in I Cor. 9:9, "Is it for the oxen that God careth?" he betrays the fact that he never lived on a farm, and that his youthful training was rabbinic. In the same situation Jesus would have said: If then God so careth for the ox of the field, how much more shall he care for the shepherds of his human flock. Jesus more than once showed an interest in the lower animals. Paul gave little thought to nature, animate or inanimate.

A different sort of survival of his Pharisaic training is found in such a passage as Gal. 3:19. The law, he writes, "was ordained through angels by the hand of a mediator." He is quoting from rabbinic tradition as though it were of equal authority with Old Testament

Scripture. Another instance is I Cor. 10:4: "They drank of a spiritual rock that followed them." We look in vain in the Old Testament for such a reference, but when we turn to the rabbinic tradition we find the teaching that the rock of Kadesh followed the Israelites in their wanderings.

Was Paul married during these years? Did he ever marry at all? The question is a difficult one. There was a rule that no one could occupy the responsible position of member of the Sanhedrin unless he had been married and had a son. Moreover, the Old Testament reflects the importance which the Jews attached to marriage. The natural inference is that Paul did marry. On the other hand, Paul implies in some passages written later that he is not married. In I Cor. 7:8 he writes: "I say to the unmarried and to widows it is good for them if they abide even as I." When Paul wrote I Corinthians he certainly was not married. The probable conclusion is that he had at one time been married, and that at the time of his missionary journeys he was a widower. That he had a high conception of the sanctity of marriage is indicated in many passages and not least by his way of referring to the church as the bride of Christ.

Under the tutorship of his experience as a Jew, Paul came to take certain fundamental positions which prepared him directly for Christian leadership. The disappointing side of the Jewish religion will be noted in the next chapter in speaking of influences leading toward his conversion. But there were three important respects in which Paul retained as a Christian the point of view of Judaism.

1. The Jewish religion stood pre-eminently for an emphasis upon purity and justice and uprightness. While it is true that the Jews had a negative and legalistic idea of righteousness, which contrasts sharply with the positive Christian outpouring of self in the service of mankind, yet they had a religion whose ethical ideals were head and shoulders above any other religion of the empire. If Paul had gone to the school of Shammai, he might have been lost in the study of ceremonial refinements and distinctions. But in the school of Hillel and Gamaliel he entered into an ethical atmosphere which amid its dialectic discussions did not entirely lose sight of the great utterances of the Hebrew prophets. "Wherewith shall I come before Jehovah? . . . . Will he be pleased with thousands of rams? . . . . What doth Jehovah require of thee but to do justly and to love kindness and to walk humbly with thy God?" (Mic. 6:6–8.)

2. The Jewish religion was reaching out into all the centers of the empire. The Pharisees had already undertaken a world-wide propaganda. At Jerusalem Paul would see evidences of this international and cosmopolitan character of Judaism. At Passover time he would notice merchants and scholars from Greece or from Alexandria worshiping beside peasants from Galilee or tentmakers from Ephesus. The list of the Passover pilgrims in Acts 2:9–11 is suggestive of the atmosphere in which Paul lived. "Parthians and Medes and Elamites, and the dwellers in Mesopotamia, in Judea and Cappadocia, in Pontus and Asia, in Phrygia and Pamphylia, in Egypt and the parts of Libya about Cyrene, and sojourners from Rome, both Jews and proselytes, Cretans

and Arabians," all were present in Jerusalem together. Many of them stayed for study or business and formed synagogues such as those listed in Acts 6:9. Paul would naturally belong to a synagogue of the Cilicians.

3. Paul's education gave him a firm conviction of the truth of monotheism. No other religion preached so effectively the doctrine that God is one, that he created the universe and holds it in the hollow of his hand. The Jewish religion was a standing protest against the already crumbling polytheism of the nations.

In his Jewish career Paul's soul was fired with these three ideas, ethical purity, the world-wide destiny of the worship of Jehovah, and its displacement of all other religions. The first led him later to despair of perfectly keeping the law; the second caused him to be deeply moved by the Hellenistic message of Stephen; the third prompted him to persecute Christians. He has been called a great volcano. One of the chief points of dispute in the school of Hillel was the question whether all kinds of fire are the same. However we decide the technical question, it is true that the same volcanic fire which in Paul's Jewish days burst forth in streams of destructive lava, afterward, when brought under the control of Christ, furnished warmth and life and light to a world that was seeking after God if haply they might find him (Acts 17:27).

4. PAUL'S PERSONAL TRAITS

There were contrasts in Paul's character. The world's leaders have often been men in whom contending forces have struggled for mastery. The more powerful the forces have been, the more powerful has been the

resultant man who has yoked them together in the
interest of one great new cause.

1. In the first place, Paul was both Jew and Roman.
Although he was a Hebrew of the Hebrews, he was born
a Roman citizen. There were those like Herod the
Great who were Roman citizens but were not pure
Jews. There were those like most of the apostles who
were pure Jews and not Roman citizens. There were
those like Lysias, the chief captain at Jerusalem, who
had "with a great sum obtained this citizenship." But
Paul was of the tribe of the beloved Benjamin and a
"Roman born." This unusual combination contributed
to his power of interpreting the gospel of Jesus to the
world. His Jewish determination and perseverance,
joined with his Roman world-inclusive vision of Christ's
mission, carried him from city to city till he met his
death at the capital of the empire.

2. Paul was both a scholar and a laboring man.
Some biographies of Paul exult in picturing him as the
greatest Christian philosophical theologian; others point
democratically to the fact that he was a man who earned
his living by manual toil. He was both. He did study
at Jerusalem with Gamaliel, probably also at the university in Tarsus. He had points of likeness with
Philo and with Seneca. He quoted Greek literature
at Athens. He understood Greek philosophy. He had
constructive genius for formulating the principles
of Christian thought. On the other hand he worked
"night and day" at his trade of tent-making to support himself. He repeatedly found himself in prison.
He was distinctly a man among men, a man of the
people. The pages of his letters remind us continually

that he was not a system or a theology, but a power and a life.

3. Paul was both a religious ascetic and a cosmopolitan leader. The monks in the secluded cloisters of the Middle Age monasteries claimed him as their model. Modern missionaries who travel around the world also point to him as the pioneer missionary. Paul buffeted his body and brought it into subjection like any monk. He went away into Arabia to meditate. He was caught up even to the third heaven and heard unspeakable words. But he came down again and spoke very plain words which brought men nearer God. The man who was capable of intensive communion with God "in Paradise" was the very man who when awakened to a world-wide responsibility had almost unlimited power in uplifting his fellow-men.

4. Paul combined physical weakness with physical strength. He suffered under great bodily handicaps. We cannot tell just what they were, but we know that his power "was made perfect in weakness." He used one attack of illness as an opportunity to preach to those who would not otherwise have heard his message (Gal. 4:13). In II Cor. 12:7 he speaks of a "thorn in the flesh, a messenger of Satan to buffet me." Many are the explanations of this thorn. The older view that his eyesight was bad was based mainly upon the statement in Gal. 4:15 that the Galatians would have plucked out their eyes and given them to him. But the reference there is probably only to giving up their most valued possession. Among the various explanations the view which most nearly fits Paul's references is that under special excitement he was subject to sudden attacks of

violent headache or dizziness, or even fainting. The thorn was given him, he says, in order that he "should not be exalted overmuch."

Yet Paul endured physical hardships which today seem incredible. On five different occasions he received thirty-nine stripes, and on three occasions he was beaten with rods. At Lystra he was stoned and left for dead. At least four times he suffered shipwreck. Once he floated about on a bit of wreckage twenty-four hours. Roman prisons were neither comfortable nor sanitary. Hunger and thirst and cold added their physical effects. Paul never spared himself. A tourist who today tries to visit all the scenes of Paul's activity is surprised at the mere distances he covered, especially in view of the comparative laboriousness of ancient travel.

Closely allied with this contrast of weakness and strength is the contrast between his care of his body and his disregard of it. His letters are full of the athletics of his day. He uses metaphors from wrestling and from racing and in general from the Greek games and from the crowning of the victors. On the other hand he said that the spirit was superior to the body. He was "of the earth, earthy," yet his "eternal" spirit was akin to God. He said to his converts: "Ye are not in the flesh but in the spirit" (Rom. 8:9). His body was only a temporary servant of his spirit. Paul lived in eternity. He showed men the way of rising superior to all earthly and physical handicaps into an exalted life of the soul.

5. Paul was a pacifist and a vigorous fighter. Peace and reconciliation are among his greatest words. His nature seems at times to have been an extremely

tender one. When he wrote a severe letter to the Corinthians it cost him many tears, as he tells in II Cor. 2:4. But he wrote it nevertheless. He often speaks affectionately of his converts as his beloved children. In his letter to the Philippians he reveals how deeply he loved them. In I Cor. 13 is the great poem on Christian love. Love is not provoked, taketh not account of evil.

Yet Paul asks those same Corinthians: "Shall I come unto you with a rod, or in a spirit of gentleness?" In II Cor. 10–13 we can almost hear the roar of cannon. "If I come again I will not spare." His irony and satire in the eleventh chapter are sharp, like a two-edged sword. In Galatians his fighting spirit can be felt on every page. "Henceforth let no man trouble me." Paul never fought for personal advantage, nor does he ever express hatred of his enemies. We feel rather that he is full of love toward those whom he must fight in the interest of Jesus' gospel of freedom and brotherhood. Yet the same man who spoke of the "peace of God which passeth understanding" and who said "love suffereth long," also said, "Put on the whole armor of God."

6. Greatest of all contrasts in Paul's nature was the combination of lowliness and exaltation. At times he was so timid that he preached "in fear and much trembling" (I Cor. 2:3). At times he felt his human frailty so keenly that he cried, "Oh wretched man that I am." When his efforts to save men seemed to fail he felt "perplexed" and "smitten down" (II Cor. 4:9). We have not only his words, "I am the least of the apostles" (I Cor. 15:9), but also his description of the apostles as

"men doomed to death" in the arena as an amusement and "a spectacle unto the world." At Ephesus he "despaired even of life" (II Cor. 1:8). He was often in the valley of the shadow of death.

On the other hand, as at Tarsus in his boyhood he had climbed the foothills for a view of the Great Sea, so in his Christian life he was led of the Spirit into exceeding high mountains. He saw the spiritual kingdoms of the world. After his experience of visiting the third heaven he could think of the earth as his footstool. To the Jews he was a Jew, to the Greeks a Greek. By the Galatians he was received as an "angel of God" (Gal. 4:14). The men of Lystra thought that he was a god come to earth (Acts 14:11). He was not a whit behind the "very chiefest apostles" (II Cor. 11:5; 12:11). He was "more than conqueror" (Rom. 8:37). The streets and walls of Tarsus dissolved in his glorified vision into the landscapes and ages of the universe. He was no longer Paul of Tarsus. He was an "ambassador" of God to propose terms of "peace" and "reconciliation" to a ravaged and yearning humanity.

SUPPLEMENTARY READING

1. Foakes-Jackson, *Saint Paul*, pp. 49–71.
2. McNeile, A. H., *St. Paul*, pp. 1–11.
3. Wood, C. T., *The Life, Letters and Religion of St. Paul*, pp. 1–12.
4. Ramsay, *St. Paul the Traveller*, pp. 29–39.
5. Kent, *Work and Teachings of the Apostles*, pp. 68–75.
6. Deissmann, *St. Paul*, pp. 57–83.
7. Gilbert, *Student's Life of Paul*, pp. 1–26.
8. Conybeare and Howson, *Life and Epistles of St. Paul*, chap. ii.
9. Bacon, *The Story of St. Paul*, pp. 13–33.
10. On Tarsus, Ramsay, *Cities of St. Paul*, pp. 85–244.

CHAPTER III

THE CALL TO SERVICE AMONG THE NATIONS

1. The Preparation
   (1) Rom. 7:7–10; Gal. 3:10
   (2) Acts 7:55—8:1; 22:20
   (3) I Cor. 15:9; Gal. 1:13, 23; Phil. 3:6; Acts 8:1–3;
      22:4, 5, 20; 26:9–11

2. The Vision
   II Cor. 4:6; I Cor. 15:8; 9:1; Gal. 1:15–17; Rom. 1:5;
   Acts 9:1–19; 22:5–16; 26:12–18

3. The Significance of the Vision
   Rom. 7:24, 25a; Rom. 1:5; Gal. 1:16; Acts 9:15;
   22:15; 26:16–18

I. THE PREPARATION

While Paul was still a "young man" certain influences and events combined to produce a most momentous revolution in his soul. He gives many hints of the preparatory forces leading toward the transition. He tells the Galatians in Gal. 1:15 that God had intended him from his birth to become his messenger to the Gentiles. In the same passage he says that God revealed his son "in" him. Similarly, in II Cor. 4:6 he says that the light "shined in our hearts." The words of Acts 26:14, "It is hard for thee to kick against the goad," suggest the persistence and effectiveness of special goading influences of which he was but dimly conscious as the time of his awakening drew near.

There is a clear difference between a transition in the soul and the first conscious realization that it is occurring

or has occurred. The transition itself may be a gradual
process. The realization may be as sudden as a flash
of lightning, and may reveal the slowly traveled road
as an instantaneous landscape view. The revealing
flash may, moreover, at the same time fire an accumulated mass of highly inflammable and even explosive
material. Three classes of such material are discernible
in Paul's pre-Christian life.

1. *Disappointment with the Jewish law.*—Chapter 7
of Romans contains the record of an intense personal
struggle. From his boyhood Paul had thought of the
Jewish law as a splendidly complete and accurate tabu-
lation of what a man must do in order to be saved. A
bright halo had gathered around it. Then came the
day in his youth when he first became conscious of the
commandment, "Thou shalt not covet." The fact that
coveting was forbidden made him interested in it.
Everyone knows the experience. He began involun-
tarily to hunt around for the objects which he ought
not to covet. The commandment wrought in him "all
manner of coveting."

>   All of pure,
> Noble, and knightly in me twined and clung
> Round that one sin.

It was but a sample of the effect of the law in general
upon him. From his coveting of his neighbor's goods he
argued that on the basis of the law he must class himself
as a sinner. The heavy negativeness of the law weighed
him down. The sunshine went out of his life. His
own words are, "I died." From that time he never
knew the full joy of living until he had the vision of
Christ risen from the dead.

While studying in Jerusalem he must have wrestled repeatedly with this problem. Some rabbis taught the consoling doctrine that if 51 per cent of a man's deeds were good, the 49 per cent of evil would be overbalanced, and ultimate salvation would be sure. But in his careful, agonizing search he concluded that one who relies upon law to save him must keep the "whole law" (Gal. 5:3). On the basis of law, what James teaches (2:10) seemed to Paul to be his own poignant experience, that whosoever shall keep the whole law and yet stumble in one point, he is guilty of all (cf. Gal. 3:10). And he felt that his own experience must be typical of all other men's. "There is none righteous, no not one." Therefore by the works of the law shall no flesh be justified. His experience under law was disappointing both in its personal effect upon his soul and in his rabbinic failure to find a theoretic system of salvation.

This was about to induce him to cast off the whole external literalistic interpretation of the law. The command "Thou shalt not covet" cannot be interpreted in terms of external deed. It is an inward and spiritual command. Perhaps he began to feel that this was a key to the only possible attitude toward the law as a whole. If the law is a unity and if part of the law is spiritual, then the only thoroughly consistent conclusion is that the whole law is to be interpreted, not as a contract to be externally observed in payment of the price of salvation, but as an inward guide to a godly life of the soul. When Paul first heard of the followers of Jesus, or at least during his continued persecution of them, he must have learned that Jesus exalted the spirit above the letter of the law. Perhaps even then he began to perceive "that the law is spiritual" (Rom. 7:14).

2. *Stephen's vision.*—Paul was a Hellenistic Jew. He was born outside of Palestine in the larger, freer atmosphere of the Hellenistic world. When he came to Jerusalem to attain that highest Jewish honor of becoming a rabbi he must have found the prevailing attitude of Jerusalem toward the rest of the empire somewhat narrow and provincial. As a Pharisee he tried, perhaps with utmost sincerity, to be whole-hearted in his loyalty to the Jewish system, to think of Jerusalem as the center of the world, to hold that when the messianic age appeared all other nations would be humiliated except in so far as they had accepted the Pharisaic regulations and become Jewish proselytes.

Perhaps he was not entirely successful in adjusting his wider experiences to the narrow view. Perhaps he began to wonder about the fate of some of his gentile classmates and friends in Tarsus and Cilicia. It may be that some seeds which Gamaliel had sown found particularly fertile soil in Paul's mind. It is in connection with the broader Hellenistic side of Paul's nature and training that the incident of Acts, chap. 7, is especially significant.

We can hardly overestimate the direct effect on Paul of Stephen's heroic martyrdom. Luke twice indicates the connection, first by saying that the witnesses laid down their garments at Paul's feet, and secondly by stating that Paul "was consenting" to his death. Moreover, who can doubt that Luke, who was of course not present at the stoning, received at least a partial account of it at some later day from the lips of his traveling companion Paul himself? When Luke paints his picture of Stephen's angelic face reflecting the glory of the opened heavens and the Son of Man standing on the right hand of God he probably paints from the palette of Paul's glowing memories. Tennyson finely expresses Stephen's look—"God's glory smote him on the face." Nor was it any ordinary experience for Paul to hear a mobbed man courageously calling with a loud voice, "Master, lay not this sin to their charge."

Strikingly suggestive also is Luke's statement in Acts 6:9 that certain of the Jews from "Cilicia" had been disputing with Stephen. Was Paul one of those who "were not able to withstand the wisdom and spirit by which he spoke?" Stephen, as his Greek name indicates, was undoubtedly a Hellenistic Jew like Paul himself. What was the new teaching which Stephen defended so ably? It was of course primarily that Jesus was the Christ. But the criminal accusation brought against him was that he spoke against Moses and the law and prophesied that the Temple and its ceremonies would pass away. The burden of the long speech which Luke ascribes to him was that the exclusiveness and cruel haughtiness of the Jewish leaders was in direct opposition to God and his Holy Spirit. Two of Paul's fundamental theses as a Christian were later transfigurations of these two propositions, first that the law was done away, and secondly that the Jew could not claim superiority to the rest of "the earth."

Stephen's pictured vision of the opened heavens and the exalted Christ, following upon his declaration of the passing of the Mosaic law and of the coming of a dispensation of the Holy Spirit, was a pattern for Paul's vision on the Damascus road. But the great apostle was still unmoved. To revert to the figure of Acts, chap. 26, he was still kicking against the goad.

3. *Persecuting the Christians.*—The reasons for which Paul "persecuted the church of God and made havoc of it" center around his position as a Pharisee. While the antagonism between Jesus and the Pharisees has perhaps sometimes been overdrawn, still as a zealous and ambitious Pharisee Paul would be quickly aroused by any criticism or revision of the law of Moses. He was naturally angered by an accusation that his fathers had "killed" the prophets. Still higher in the scale of blasphemy was the Christian teaching that God had rejected the Pharisees and that the magnificent temple ritual was to be done away. Finally, as the climax of it all, this new sect claimed that the Jesus of Nazareth who called the Pharisees hypocrites was the long-hoped-for Messiah, God's anointed King of Israel. Following or supporting a false Messiah was a crime punishable by death. Paul's hatred was kindled by the Christian exclusion of the Pharisees from heaven, while his determined program of persecution was sustained by what seemed to him a meritorious loyalty to the traditions of his fathers. Christians were in a sense traitors to the law and the Temple.

During his persecution Paul saw much of the Christian spirit. He probably saw more than any other unbaptized man. He saw the disciples at the times when their faith was on trial, when he shut them up "in prisons," when he gave his vote against them, when he strove to make them blaspheme. Moreover, "entering into every house" he must have seen them in the midst of their Christian worship and brotherly service.

The Christian rite of baptism, of which he must have known, symbolized the washing away of sin. It was far more impressive than the ceremonial washings of the Jews which were performed in fulfilment of laws of purification. Christian baptism symbolized a freeing of the soul from evil deeds and evil thoughts. Paul's experience with law and the sense of sin which it created prepared him for an appreciation of this cleansing rite. Later on, in Rom. 6:3, 4, he speaks of baptism as symbolizing death and burial with Christ, leading to a rising with him in newness of life. If Paul, as he expresses it, had already "died" under the law even while the tremendous inertia of his powerful soul kept him still fighting for it, the Christian symbol of baptism with its suggestion of dying and rising again would make a strong appeal.

Often Paul must have stumbled upon the common meal which the Christians celebrated in memory of Christ's Last Supper. There he found the poor and the well-to-do gathered round a common table. This Christian "love feast," as they called it, stood for the brotherhood and equality which is in Christ. There was no distinction between one Christian and another. Certainly in theory, if not always in practice, this common repast symbolized that larger brotherhood of man for which Stephen had died and which Paul of Tarsus, the Roman citizen, would feel belonged to the highest conception of Jehovah's will for man.

Paul's active persecution of the Christians, resulting from a combination of his Pharisaic aspirations with his energetic disposition, was carried on quite regardless of the rumblings of the inner storm which was about to break. As so fitly expressed in the story of Jean Valjean, he was "doing an act of which he was no longer capable." Moreover, it is a truth not confined to the ministry of Jesus that a demon before he is expelled from a man is particularly active during the last moments of occupation. "Straightway the spirit tare him and he fell on the ground and wallowed foaming" (Mark 9:20). And so it was that Paul, as Luke expresses it, was still "breathing threatening and slaughter."

2. THE VISION

The influences which had been gathering around Paul had produced as yet no consciously decisive impression. But on that momentous journey from Jerusalem to Damascus the whole direction of his career was changed. Occasional flashes in his letters illumine for us his vivid memory of the great event. Most suggestive of all are the words in II Cor. 4:6. The same God who in the beginning created the light out of the darkness of chaos "shined in our (my) heart" and he saw "the face of Jesus Christ" radiant with "the glory of God."

This transforming vision which engraved "the face of Jesus" upon his soul took place at or near Damascus (Gal. 1:16, 17). In the vision Jesus was revealed to him as the Son of God (Gal. 1:12, 16). The experience was sudden, overwhelming, revolutionary. He had been one who "persecuted the church of God and made havoc of it." But "straightway" after the event he went away into Arabia (Gal. 1:13, 16, 17). It was a work of God, whose "good pleasure" it was to make the revelation (Gal. 1:15). That he had "seen Jesus" is attested by many references. In I Cor. 9:1 Paul asks, "Have I not seen Jesus our Lord?" In I Cor. 15:8, in listing the appearances of the risen Jesus to the disciples, he writes: "And last of all as to the child untimely born he appeared to me also." In Rom. 1:5 he says that his commission of apostleship among the nations was received through Jesus Christ. In Phil. 3:12 he writes in graphic metaphor that he "was laid hold on by Christ Jesus" as a prize is taken by a victor in an athletic contest.

The Book of Acts contains three accounts of the conversion. While two of these are included in speeches attributed to Paul, the details of expression are best regarded as the work of the author or his source. In comparison with the references in Paul's letters the Acts accounts are in some ways disappointing, as in the omission of any reference to the face of Jesus, while on the other hand they contribute several additional items of information, such as that the event took place "about noon" (Acts 22:6; 26:13). The items which are found in all three accounts may be regarded as the most important elements in the Acts description. (1) All three Acts accounts record that the event took place on the way to Damascus. (2) In all three accounts is the statement that there was a light. Just how far the light affected the companions of Paul is somewhat uncertain. In chapter 9 a light out of heaven shone "round about him"; in chapter 22 his companions "beheld the light" which shone round about Paul; in chapter 26 the light shone round about the companions also. In chapter 9 the light apparently had no great effect upon the companions who "stood" listening to the voice, while in chapter 26 the light was so brilliant that they "were all fallen" to the earth before Paul heard the voice. (3) All three accounts state that Paul heard a voice saying, "I am Jesus." How far this voice was externally audible to others is again uncertain, chapter 9 speaking of the companions as "hearing the voice," and chapter 22 stating that "they heard not the voice." If Luke had been asked by some reader why he allowed such different expressions to stand in the accounts, he would perhaps have answered that the companions heard what Paul recognized as a voice, but they did not hear any words nor recognize it as a voice. Very suggestive in this connection is the statement of John 12:29 that the multitude which stood by when the Greeks came to Jesus "said that it thundered; others said, An angel hath spoken to him." (4) Finally, all three accounts indicate that it was no mere appearance of a physical man claiming to be Jesus. It was a "heavenly vision" (Acts 26:19) which Paul saw.

These items which Luke three times records show where he laid the emphasis. The indefiniteness in regard to the effect upon the companions was due partly to Luke's use of different sources, but partly also to Luke's unconcern for minor details generally. The great central fact was that Paul was a changed man, that one day while on a mission of persecution to Damascus a great light had suddenly fallen upon him in which he saw a heavenly vision of one who revealed himself by saying, "I am Jesus," and whom Paul straightway acknowledged as Lord.

There are several other items narrated in one or another of the three accounts. In Acts, chap. 9, it is stated that the duration of the blindness was three days. The three days' fasting, the vision to Ananias, the laying on of hands by Ananias that he might be filled with the Holy Spirit, the falling of scales from Paul's eyes—all these are from chapter 9. In chapter 22 Ananias is represented as giving the commission to Paul: "Thou shalt be a witness for him unto all men"; in chapter 26, where Ananias is not mentioned, the commission is naturally given as from Jesus himself: "To this end have I appeared unto thee to appoint thee a minister and a witness."

Paul's own statements taken together with the statements which Luke gives in threefold form disclose the essential heart of the great event. Paul, the Pharisee, the determined persecutor of the Christian church, was suddenly arrested near Damascus by a vision of Jesus as the Son of God. The vision was of such a nature as to convince him that Jesus was alive and enthroned as Lord, the Son of God, with power. God, through Christ, laid hold on Paul's soul. Henceforth Christ occupied the center of his consciousness. "To me to live is Christ."

The external landscape through which Paul passed on that momentous journey is in some ways a commentary on the experience itself. It is perhaps fanciful to see any direct connection between the two. And yet they belong together as a frame belongs to a picture.

Jerusalem is a barren, rocky place by nature. Vegetation is scanty. Damascus is a luxuriant oasis. To the west of it are the mountains of Hermon with the fields of snow. A copious river, fed by the snows of Hermon, flows down into the rich soil of the great desert and spends itself in one prodigal burst of fertility and fruitfulness. Viewing the spot from a nearby summit, the prophet Mohammed said that as he expected to have only once the experience of entering paradise he would stay outside this city.

Setting out from Jerusalem along the road to Damascus, Paul first followed the ridge northward through Judea and Samaria, passing many landmarks of Israel's history. Then entering the plain of Esdraelon, where the caravans of the nations were continually passing, he came down to the Jordan just south of the Sea of Galilee. He crossed the Jordan at a depression of 700 feet below sea-level, then entered the dark canyon-like gorge of the Yarmuk. Tediously in this veritable valley of the shadow of death he climbed the ascending road till he quite suddenly emerged upon the high free plateau which stretched away toward Damascus. There at an altitude of nearly 3,000 feet, perhaps within sight of the city which bears a "new fruit every month" (cf. Ezek. 47:12), God touched his soul, showed him the vision, and called him to the task. As the significance of the experience gradually unfolded itself to him in the hours· and days that followed, it had three distinct elements: Christ, the nations, and his own apostleship.

3. THE SIGNIFICANCE OF THE VISION

1. The conversion was a personal conviction that Jesus was alive. He had heard the wonderful tales about the resurrection, but he had believed none of them. Now he was convinced that they were true. Never again did he doubt the resurrection. But not only was Jesus alive; he was the Son of God, object of God's

love, revelation of his goodness. All Paul's later Christian teaching gathered around this truth, that the crucified Jesus had appeared to him in the glory of exaltation to the right hand of God. Even greater than the mental conviction was the spiritual conviction of hope for his own soul. He who had died under law might follow the guiding hand of Christ out of death into a new life of spiritual freedom.

2. In the conversion was included a conviction that the truth he had learned was for all nations. They are mentioned repeatedly in Paul's allusions (Rom. 1:5; Gal. 1:16; cf. I Cor. 9:1; 15:8 ff.) and in all three accounts of Acts (26:17; 9:15; 22:15). Christ appealed not merely to Paul's experience as a Jew seeking personal salvation, but also to his Greek nature as a man of Tarsus. The vision was no mere individual or even national affair. Paul saw the gates of the kingdom thrown wide open. Palestinian Jewish exclusiveness was gone. The promise to Abraham and to his seed was meant for Jews and Greeks alike, for Barbarians and Scythians also. This picture of a redeemed and glorified humanity living in a new world of peace and brotherhood, this thought that Jesus and his gospel were to be preached among all the nations, was the second element in the glory of his vision.

3. The third element was his own relation to this international destiny of the gospel. He was himself to be the instrument in God's hand of bringing about this great end. Through the risen Jesus he "received . . . . apostleship . . . . among all the nations" (Rom. 1:5). God's purpose in revealing his Son in him, he writes in Gal. 1:16, was "that I might preach him among the

Gentiles." "To this end have I appeared unto thee, to appoint thee a minister and a witness" unto the nations "to open their eyes that they may turn from darkness to light" (Acts 26:16-18). He was himself to lead in the spiritual conquest of the world. This was an appeal to his Roman nature.

His apostleship among the nations did not, of course, mean that he was to go exclusively or primarily into non-Jewish circles. He was not to go over the heads of the Jews of the Dispersion or to ignore them. On the contrary his plan was naturally to preach to the Jews in the various cities and, through conversion of them, so to multiply his efforts that the Gentiles should be brought into a great international Christian organization similar to the powerful Jewish one.

In the light of his later methods it is possible to detect a further and supreme element in his thought of his own practical relation to the great program. There dawned suddenly or gradually upon him a vision of a particular way in which the international mission might be effectively put into operation. He saw the key by which the heavy door separating Jew from Gentile might in Christ be unlocked and swung wide open. Whether he saw it suddenly on the road to Damascus, whether it was a primal cause and part of his conversion, or whether he searched it out gradually in the later days in Arabia or still later in actual experience on missionary journeys is not a matter of vital consequence. It was in any case a primary element in the making of Paul into the greatest of the apostles. This key he found in the peculiar situation existing in the synagogues of the Dispersion.

In the synagogues throughout the world were those "devout" men who "feared God," as mentioned so often in the Book of Acts. They were eager to accept the monotheistic message of Judaism, but were not willing to obey Jewish ceremonial requirements, such as circumcision and not eating with Gentiles. Now the gospel of Jesus, including all that was good in Judaism and none of these objectionable features, freed from the Jewish atmosphere of Palestine and carried through the synagogues of the world, would quickly kindle and rapidly spread among that outer circle of devout Gentiles in the synagogues, and from them would set on fire the nations of the world. When this strategic advantage of the gospel first flashed upon Paul the Roman citizen, he must have trembled with the anticipation of a vast victory almost accomplished.

The conversion, then, had its three great parts—the personal conviction, the circle of the nations, and the practical program. The first was Jewish, the second was Greek, and the third was Roman. The first was related to his experience under law; the second, to Stephen's vision; and the third, to his life as a persecuting apostle of Judaism.

The exaltation of heart and soul, which gradually came over Paul after the great vision, finds expression in a multitude of ways in his letters. He had been trying to find his way in the "darkness" of night and was now rejoicing "in the light" of a new dawn. His former life was like "bondage" compared to the new "freedom." His Jerusalem existence was like that of men who are at "enmity" as compared with the Damascus experience of "reconciliation." At Jerusalem he felt himself under "condemnation," and the "judgment" was "death," but at Damascus he was "justified." Christ had made "intercession" and brought about the "justification." He was received by "adoption" into a new family in which Christ was the firstborn among many brethren. God made a "new covenant" with him very different from the old one. His were the "riches" of God's "goodness" and knowledge. He was no longer alone. But, provided with a sure "breast-plate" and "helmet" and a whole "armor," he was enlisted in the great new cause of God among the nations of the world.

SUPPLEMENTARY READING

1. Foakes-Jackson, *Saint Paul*, pp. 72–82.
2. McNeile, A. H., *St. Paul*, pp. 11–17.
3. Wood, C. T., *The Life of Paul*, pp. 13–25.
4. Farrar, *Life and Work of St. Paul*, chap. x.
5. Burton, *Saul's Experience on the Way to Damascus* (1896).
6. Kent, *Work and Teachings of the Apostles*, pp. 75–78.
7. Gilbert, *Student's Life of Paul*, pp. 27–41.
8. Conybeare and Howson, *Life and Epistles of St. Paul*, chap. iii.
9. Matheson, *Spiritual Development of St. Paul*, pp. 22–64.
10. Gardner, *Religious Experiences of St. Paul*, pp. 20–56.
11. *Bible for Home and School*, "Acts," pp. 99–103.
12. Bacon, *The Story of St. Paul*, pp. 34–67.
13. Cone, *Paul the Man, the Missionary, and the Teacher*, pp. 53–66.

CHAPTER IV

YEARS OF ADJUSTMENT

1. IN DAMASCUS AND ARABIA

In moments of vision men see far-reaching ambitions accomplished on a large scale, while the smaller details of the immediate means of accomplishment may still lie in obscurity. God "revealed his Son" in Paul that he "might preach him among the Gentiles." Yet after his baptism by Ananias, Paul hastened away into retirement. "Straightway I conferred not with flesh and blood," he says (Gal. 1:16), "but I went away into Arabia." Moses, Elijah, Luther, Savonarola, all knew what it meant to go away for a while into retirement. Jesus, too, went away into "the wilderness" immediately after his baptism. Paul needed to adjust himself to his new situation, to think over the meaning of his call to Christian discipleship and to missionary leadership. It would naturally require considerable time to formulate even in a general way the terms in which he might interpret the gospel of the Jewish Messiah to the nations of the empire.

59

Inasmuch as Paul was a man accustomed to city life, it is not impossible that he sought out some city as his stopping-place in Arabia. Possibly, too, he did some preaching there to test the effect of his gospel.

The most marvelous ruin of an ancient city in Arabia, perhaps the most extraordinary and unusual in the world, is the city of Petra, in Arabia Petraea, of which Aretas IV (II Cor. 11:32) was king. Situated to the east and south of the Dead Sea, it has escaped very largely the destructive visits of passing armies. Two rocky valleys or gorges cross each other there at right angles. Temples and other buildings were not built, but hollowed out of the sandstone walls. Columns, friezes, façades, gables, portals, were not set in place, but left in place by carving away the rock around them. About seven hundred and fifty such edifices are still in fairly good condition, many of them almost as good as on the day the artist finished them. The "monastery," as it is called, has a front approximately 150 feet wide and 150 feet high. How instructive, too, to stand before a small madonna thus carved into the rock and in another niche beside it a similarly created cross! Such a place has a great speculative interest as suggestive of where Paul may have been when in Arabia.

Three years he spent in Arabia and Damascus. Since the Jews seem to have been very antagonistic in Damascus, it is probable that he spent the larger part of the time in Arabia. Then he went back again to Damascus.

Luke betrays no knowledge of the sojourn in Arabia. He narrates that Paul spent "certain days" at Damascus and "proclaimed Jesus" in the synagogues. In all probability the preaching in the synagogues occurred after the return from Arabia, just as in the ministry of Jesus the wilderness experience preceded his preaching. His final departure from Damascus was hastened by the intense hostility among the Jews of the city. His international vision threatened the religious supremacy and prerogative of the Jews. They were only too quick to see it. As he "increased in strength they took counsel to kill him." This was the beginning of his humiliations. Up to this time as Jew and as Christian he had been outwardly proud and dignified. Now he was to learn that the Christian strength is made perfect only in endurance. How deep and lasting an impression his first humiliation made upon him is indicated not only by the probability that he told Luke the details of it (Acts 9:24, 25), but especially by the fact that it is the only persecution which he himself gives with definite mention of time, place, and person in the well-known list of his hardships. "Through a window was I let down in a basket by the wall and escaped his hands" (II Cor. 11:33).

2. IN JERUSALEM AND SYRIA AND CILICIA

Concerning Paul's visit to Jerusalem at this time, Paul's own words in Galatians are quite explicit. He says in regard to his gospel: "Neither did I receive it from man, nor was I taught it. . . . . After three years I went up to Jerusalem to visit Cephas and tarried with him fifteen days. But other of the apostles saw I none, save James the Lord's brother" (Gal. 1:12, 18, 19).

He did not go up to Jerusalem to receive instruction from the apostles as to their idea of Jesus' gospel. He had a program which far exceeded their little plans for winning the Jews. He was careful not to be influenced by them in such a way as to lose the glory of his vision or become a merely second-hand apostle. While they were preaching as far as Samaria or Joppa he was in imagination already visiting Cilicia and the realms beyond.

Nevertheless he wished to make the personal acquaintance of Peter, the chief apostle, and of James, the head of the Jerusalem church, Jesus' own brother. He tarried only fifteen days. Luke states that it was Barnabas who trusted Paul in the face of the general suspicion, and who introduced him to the apostles—that same Barnabas who afterward led the way on the first missionary journey. Luke also says that Paul preached boldly in the name of Jesus, but this preaching could not have been very extended, since Paul writes (Gal. 1:22) that when he came into the regions of Syria and Cilicia he "was still unknown by face unto the churches of Judea." Paul did not wish to be drawn into the Jerusalem work. His high vision held him true to his larger mission. The great leaders in every age are those who see a great goal and constantly, persistently push toward it. Paul's ambition was so large and his consciousness of it and loyalty to it so intense that he was exalted above every opposition. While they were seeking to. kill him at Jerusalem (Acts 9:29) he was listening to those words spoken to him in a trance (Acts 22:17, 21): "Depart, for I will send thee forth far hence unto the Gentiles."

He started. Tarsus was his goal. Those new friends whom he would now, after the example of Christ, call "brothers" accompanied him as far as Caesarea. He departed, probably by ship and alone on his mission. He was returning homeward. Perhaps in Tarsus itself he would be rejected as Jesus was at Nazareth. Yet in his own country of Cilicia, which he knew so well, he would have excellent opportunity to develop his powers in preaching the gospel.

Imagine a Buddhist student who has come from Japan to continue his higher studies in an American college. He hears the call of God. Christ grips his soul. He is chosen to bring the oriental world into the Kingdom. The greatness of the vision makes him a new man. He will spend a time longer in studying the foundations of Christianity. Then he will hasten back to Japan. He knows the language; he is familiar with the customs; he can associate with the people of his race and tell them directly and effectively his message of a new Orient in Christ.

Even so was Paul a power in Tarsus and Cilicia. How long he stayed in Tarsus, whether he undertook further studies in the university, what success attended his efforts in presenting the gospel, what friends he lost, what others he gained, whether there were times of discouragement and despair—on all these and many other matters the record is silent. Did he sometimes leave his difficulties for a while and climb up into the heights of those nearby Taurus Mountains which he had loved in his boyhood? When he was upon the height alone with his God was his vision renewed? Did his eyes fall upon a world expectant and waiting for its redemption? Did he come back to his task with fresh courage and larger hope? Did he thus during these years develop a spiritual brawn and moral muscle which should enable him to perform those marvelous feats of later years?

In reckoning the number of years he spent in and around Tarsus we must be guided by Paul's remark in Gal. 2:1, that "after the space of fourteen years" he went up again to Jerusalem with Barnabas, taking Titus. This visit to Jerusalem occurred after the first missionary journey, as will be explained on a later page. If we reckon the Antioch ministry at about two years and the first missionary tour at two years, then subtract the three years spent in Damascus and Arabia, we may conclude that he was about seven years in Tarsus and the neighboring "regions of Syria and Cilicia" (Gal. 1:21).

There are three further bits of information which may be connected with these years. (1) His labors were not all in vain, for in Acts 15:41 we read that "he went through Syria and Cilicia confirming the churches." It must have been a source of joy to find that the churches he had formed were still thriving, needing only to be "confirmed" in their faith. (2) In these years occurred probably many of the tests of his faith which he lists in II Cor. 11:23–33—shipwreck, imprisonment, flogging, perils of robbers, perils in the city, perils in the wilderness, cold and nakedness, hunger and thirst, and last but not least the daily anxiety for the permanence of his work. (3) Reckoning back "fourteen years ago" from the time he wrote II Corinthians it becomes evident that it was about the middle of the Tarsus sojourn that Paul had the experience which he describes in II Cor. 12:2–4. He was "caught up into paradise" and heard "unspeakable words." Just what new revelation God gave him he does not state. But it must have included a higher, larger, clearer conception of the majesty of Christ and of the meaning of his own apostleship among the nations.

3. AT ANTIOCH

The city of Antioch, located at the northeast corner of the Mediterranean, about fifteen miles from the coast, was one of the largest and proudest cities of the empire. The river Orontes flows past the base of Mount Silvius. Protected on the one side by the river and on the other side by the mountain, the city of Antioch grew to be a great center, not only of political life but of industry and art. The Syrian kings from the time of Antiochus IV had their palaces there. When the Roman armies overran the East, Antioch bought its freedom by payment of money and the Roman governor took up his residence there.

The massive walls of the city extended up over the ridge of the mountain. From the highest point one can today look down upon the roofs of the modern city, which has shrunk to such an extent that it seems to be almost lost in the great area inclosed by the ancient wall. There may have been something like half a million people in and around the city. Josephus says there were only two larger cities in the empire, Rome and Alexandria. As we look down upon those modern roofs we are disappointed not to see any of the polished marble columns with which Herod the Great ornamented both sides of the main street for a distance of some miles. At a little distance from the city is "that sweet grove of Daphne by Orontes" (*Paradise Lost*, Book IV, l. 272). This marvelous little natural park, used as the scene of many modern pieces of fiction, was also in antiquity the center of much legend and story. In Paul's time no doubt thousands came to see the profusion of waterfalls among the rocks and the trees.

Fifteen miles away on the coast was Seleucia, the seaport of Antioch. Here too are eloquent remains of the civilization amid which Paul began his first formal missionary work There is the great dam, built across the mountain stream which threatened the town during sudden, heavy storms. Any idea that Paul lived in an antiquated and darkened age may be dispelled by an inspection of this piece of masonry or by climbing up around behind the dam and walking through the rock tunnel 21 feet wide and 21 feet high, constructed to carry away the water which collected in time of flood, diverting it through the mountain and emptying it into the sea about 1,200 yards away. Near by is the massive Roman pier, called "the pier of St. Paul," built so carefully and of such huge blocks of stone that a large section of it still remains, running out into the waves of the Mediterranean and pointing silently, steadily westward. Upon these great blocks Paul may often have stood and, looking out to sea, have had an earlier, dimmer view of the Macedonian vision and have heard men of every race saying, "Come over and help us."

The origin of the Christian community in Antioch is given in Acts 11:19, 20. It was the product of two influences. In the first place we see the effect of the death of Stephen, that first martyr, who did more in his death than in his life, for the persecution served to spread the fire which was burning in the hearts of the early disciples. Many of them came to Antioch and convinced the Jews there of the messiahship of Jesus, founding a Jewish-Christian community. On the other hand there were some, men of Cyprus and Cyrene, who came to Antioch and spoke directly to "the Greeks" and persuaded them to accept the revelation of Jesus. While the reading "Greeks" (vs. 20) is not quite certain, the context indicates a distinct Greek movement outside the synagogue. This movement among the Greeks, independent of the Jews, afforded a peculiarly practical opportunity for Paul's universalism on a later occasion.

Meanwhile the church at Jerusalem, hearing of the Christian activity in Antioch, felt that a leader should be sent who could give a correct version of the teaching concerning Jesus, and who could bring the new community into a bond of union with the central one at Jerusalem. It does not appear that in sending Barnabas they were assuming official control of the church in Antioch. Their thought was rather to guide and to help. Barnabas was wise and prudent and full of the Spirit. Hence it was that much people were added unto the Lord in Antioch, and hence it was that Barnabas, finding his hands full and looking about for assistance, went to Tarsus to find Paul.

Barnabas' special reason for wanting assistance may possibly have been that the two circles of Christians in Antioch created a difficulty for him. At first the Jewish Christians may have been hesitant about associating too closely with Gentiles, especially in the eating of the Lord's Supper. There was need of extreme tact. Perhaps at first there would even be scruples against

Barnabas eating now with the gentile Christians and now with the Jews. If Barnabas and Paul could work together, Barnabas more particularly with the Jews and Paul more particularly with the Gentiles, there was every reason to hope that ideals of Christian brotherhood might be preserved. Suggestions of the difficulties which might arise we may find in the Cornelius incident of Acts, chap. 10, and in the later experience of Peter at Antioch, narrated in Gal. 2:11–13.

Barnabas had taken particular interest in Paul during the first visit of the latter to Jerusalem on the return from Damascus (Acts 9:27). He saw in him the possibilities of a great leader. Paul may have told Barnabas that Christ had called him that he "might preach him among the Gentiles" (Gal. 1:16). He may have told him further of the vision in the Temple (Acts 22:17, 18) and of his commission of apostleship to "all the nations" (Rom. 1:5). All these years Barnabas had undoubtedly kept himself informed concerning this fiery young man from Tarsus who had such remarkable visions and such persevering activity. He now realized that Paul was the one man to help him with the Greek half of the Antioch responsibility.

For a whole year they worked together with splendid success. For a year Paul handled the problems of transferring the Jewish gospel to the Gentiles. Perhaps under the expert local advice of Barnabas he was able to avoid mistakes of previous years. Nowhere was the Jew-Gentile problem more delicate than in Antioch. In many other ways also the year must have been of significance to Paul. Probably Barnabas told him much of Jesus and the early apostles during this time. Certainly their joint success gave shape and reality to Paul's missionary ambition which was soon to bear fruit in a large and definite way.

A primary indication of the success at Antioch is the fact that Christians were here first recognized as a distinct and separate sect. Here for the first time the disciples were called "Christians." The form of Luke's statement, "were called," shows that the name was first applied to the company of disciples by non-Christian outsiders. Much has been written concerning the significance of this appellation. Two points are especially noteworthy.

1. As a distinctive epithet the name was of gentile, not Jewish, origin. If Jews had called the disciples "Christians" they would in a way have been admitting that Jesus was the Christ. The Jews in speaking of the disciples would naturally call them "followers of Jesus." In any case among Jews the title "Christians," i.e., "followers of the Messiah," would not be distinctive. There were and had been many sects claiming for their leaders the title Messiah. The reference might be to any of these. The Gentiles, on the other hand, were probably familiar with only one sect, the followers of Jesus, which held that the Messiah had appeared. It was because this particular messianic movement spread beyond the Jews that the name "Christians" was, to the Gentiles, a new and distinguishing term. It probably arose in immediate connection with Paul's own work in Antioch. When the name later became one of the great words of the empire Paul could take no little pride in telling his comrade Luke that *his* Christians were the first "Christians" in the world.

2. The Greek word *chrestos* ("good, useful") was pronounced almost like *Christos* ("Christ"). "Christians" is found in inscriptions and elsewhere spelled "Chrestians." Possibly the name was originally a bit of slang. Very likely it was sometimes used in ridicule. We might approach the pun in English, especially in a time of war, by slurringly speaking of certain "sons of the Revolution" as the "suns of the Revolution." The "Christians" were not merely those who proclaimed Jesus as the "Christ"; they may also have been the "goody-goodies" of the wags of Antioch.

4. RELIEVING THE FAMINE AT JERUSALEM

After Paul had been in Antioch about a year, one of those prophets who were so common in the Orient predicted that the price of grain was to rise so high that the poorer Christians at Jerusalem would suffer unless relieved. Suetonius speaks of these high prices under Claudius. Eusebius and others mention the scarcity of food in various localities. It was a similar situation to that caused by the world-war in our own time. But under Claudius the famine was probably not as acute as in some localities in the modern day, and was caused not by war but by scarcity of rainfall. It is probable that Agabus either had a wide knowledge of the food situation or else simply enough agricultural common sense to realize that one or two seasons of scanty rain meant scarcity of grain. His Christian spirit prompted him to declare the situation which would arise in Jerusalem and to urge preparation for relief.

The absence of any statement in Gal. 1:18—2:1 concerning any visit of Paul to Jerusalem at this time constitutes a real difficulty in the Acts account. In Galatians Paul is saying how little he had seen of the Jerusalem Christian leaders. It is hard to believe he would omit a visit in such a recital. Perhaps the fact that Luke does not explicitly narrate the arrival of Paul personally in Jerusalem and does not narrate any experience of Paul while there reflects an uncertainty or lack of information on this particular point. It seems best to conclude that although the responsibility of bringing relief was laid upon Paul and Barnabas, and these two labored together in the good work, nevertheless Paul himself probably did not go all the way to Jerusalem.

The significance of this brotherly help extended by the Antioch church should not be overlooked. It had its larger importance along three different lines.

1. It was the first step toward internationalizing the fund administered by the deacons with Stephen as chairman. The same word "ministration" is used in both cases (Acts 6:1; 12:25). It was a broadening of that early Christian idea of the community of goods. It was putting into deeds that larger brotherhood symbolized in the celebration of the Lord's Supper. It was the harbinger of that "ministering" to the saints (II Cor. 9:1) for which Paul later gathered contributions from all his churches.

2. The act paved the way for exchange of good feeling between the churches of Antioch and Jerusalem. It postponed the difficult day of Acts, chap. 15, in which the question of the relation of Jew and Gentile in Christ became acute. Every seed of fellowship planted now yielded sixty and a hundred fold at that conference in which Paul pleaded for the Gentiles.

3. Paul and Barnabas were associated together in this enterprise. Who can doubt that this in a special way hastened the larger missionary enterprise upon which they so soon afterward embarked? The relationship is made still more probable by the appearance of John Mark, who joined them at this time (Acts 12:25).

These twelve years we have called years of adjustment. Three years of comparative seclusion in Arabia and Damascus, seven years of work in Tarsus and Cilicia, a year and probably most of a second year of inspiring success with Barnabas in Antioch made up the education by which the converted Pharisee became the splendid leader who was now about to embark upon the first great missionary adventure. During these years the hot iron of Paul's nature had been tempered into steel, and the brightness of the glory of the conversion sobered by the hard facts of persecution and indifference. Many have felt that they must think of the Damascus vision as a small one in order to allow for a continued growth and expansion during these years. But biography teaches that often the inventor, the reformer, the pioneer, see more in a moment than they can accomplish in a lifetime. Their vision is their power. From time to time in the midst of hard labor the vision is renewed. At Jerusalem in the Temple in a trance Paul had heard again the commission, "I will send thee forth far hence unto the Gentiles" (Acts 22:21). In the midst of his prosaic labors around Tarsus he had been at one time, as already noted, "caught up even to the third heaven" and had "heard unspeakable words" (II Cor. 12:2, 4). Through all these years he had been attaining the power to "turn the world upside down," to revolve the great sphere of humanity "from darkness to light" and from the night of the "power of Satan" to the dawn of the Sun of Righteousness.

SUPPLEMENTARY READING

1. Foakes-Jackson, *Saint Paul*, pp. 83–85.
2. McNeile, A. H., *St. Paul*, pp. 17–28.
3. Wood, C. T., *The Life of Paul*, pp. 26–45.
4. Ramsay, *St. Paul the Traveller*, pp. 40–69.
5. Kent, *Work and Teachings of the Apostles*, pp. 78–80, 85–86.
6. Gilbert, *Student's Life of Paul*, pp. 42–68.
7. Conybeare and Howson, *Life and Epistles of St. Paul*, chap. iv.
8. Farrar, *Life and Work of St. Paul*, chap. xi.
9. *Bible for Home and School*, "Acts," pp. 103–6, 121–24, 130.
10. McGiffert, *A History of Christianity in the Apostolic Age*, pp. 161–72.
11. Bacon, *The Story of St. Paul*, pp. 68–97.

CHAPTER V

A CAMPAIGN WITH BARNABAS

1. PAUL'S PLAN OF ADVANCE

A study of the record of Paul's missionary activities shows that he pursued a definite, well-thought-out, and far-reaching policy. It was not enough for him to preach here and there as he found opportunity. The planting of the new religion throughout the length of the Roman Empire became his all-inclusive ambition. This involved four things.

1. One element in his plan was the selection of the strategic points of the empire as the places of his activity. There are in our New Testament names of many places which cannot be located with certainty. But the names of the cities where Paul worked stand out in large, clear letters on our maps. Where life was thickest and fastest, where history was being made, in the centers of commerce and influence, he spent the rapid years of his career. The modern railroads touch these same centers. The

74

extensive ruins indicate that they were far greater in that day than today.

2. After selection of strategic points the next step in his plan was the establishment of Christian communities in these cities and the nourishment of them into strength sufficient to enable them to stand alone. It was not enough to proclaim the message or simply to gather a group of converts. The infant community must be developed into power and permanence.

3. A third item in the program was the leaving of the surrounding regions to be reached from these centers. Although he thought and planned largely in terms of provinces, he knew the big city was the key to the province. Epaenetus was the first-fruits "of Asia" (Rom. 16:5), although he was probably a convert of Ephesus. From Ephesus the work spread, as Paul planned, into the neighboring cities. He personally knew the man in whose house the Christians met at Laodicea (Col. 4:15). Paul's fellow-worker Epaphras was a man of Colossae (Col. 4:12, 13).

4. His plan involved the extension of his own efforts through Asia Minor, Greece, Italy, and even Spain; in short the covering of the empire from Jerusalem westward with a chain of churches located in the strategic centers of population. What the world owes to this farseeing plan of the apostle and the efforts that he put forth for its materialization taxes one's imagination to estimate.

The realization of this great plan he felt as a peculiar "necessity laid" upon him. Because the vision had been given to him more clearly than to any other he felt that he was "a debtor" to carry the good news "both to the Greeks and to the Barbarians." Although he was the "least of the apostles" and "not worthy to be called an apostle," the clearness of his plan gave him confidence. The glowing sense of his mission paralleled in intensity that of any other great benefactor of mankind. He was a David Livingstone, with the height and depth and breadth of Livingstone's soul, sent not to "darkest Africa," but to the most enlightened cities of his world. When Paul set out upon a missionary tour with Barnabas he soon outgrew his companion. Even the young man Mark could not keep pace with him, but turned back home.

2. ON THE ISLAND OF CYPRUS

From the stone pier at Seleucia, the harbor of Antioch, Barnabas and Paul sailed forth. Although Luke narrates that they were sent by certain men in the church at Antioch, Paul's apostleship does not date from this time. Paul was an apostle, "not from men, neither through man." His apostleship dated from his conversion.

Nevertheless the Christian church was now possessed of a new spirit. Luke begins here a new section in his Book of Acts. Thus far Christianity had been in Jewish hands. The rest of the Book of Acts concerns the gospel among the Gentiles. These men, Barnabas and Paul, as they voyage away, introduce a new epoch. The thought which we find expressed so often in the Old Testament, that the people of Jehovah should have no dealings with the peoples of the earth, has given way to the spirit of Jesus' parable concerning the man who hid his talent in a napkin. That most vital difference

of Jesus' teaching from the teaching of the Jews, the
positive emphasis upon the service of humanity, finds
deep and clear expression on board that boat as the pier
of Seleucia fades away and the mountain citadel óf
Antioch sinks toward the horizon.

This first formal enterprise was not in the nature of a
wild experiment. Barnabas was himself a native of
Cyprus, as we learn from Acts 4:36. Moreover, Acts
11:19 states that the gospel had already been preached
there by those who had been "scattered abroad" at the
death of Stephen. Mark also, the cousin of Barnabas
(not nephew of Barnabas, as sometimes translated),
would naturally have relatives in Cyprus, although his
home was in Jerusalem, where his mother had a good-
sized house (Acts 12:12). This John Mark was the same
man who long afterward wrote the Gospel of Mark.
Whether he joined the other two at Salamis or whether
he had been with them from Antioch is not quite clear.
The probability is that he was with them all along, and
that it was because he was not specially delegated by the
church that he was not mentioned by Luke at the start.

In the tour of Cyprus there are four items of importance.

1. The tour was not a small or hasty piece of work.
The voyage from Antioch to Cyprus, about 140 miles,
was made in a little, ancient, wooden sailing vessel. Nor
was there any modern railway to carry them the 100
miles which separated Salamis at one end of the island
from Paphos at the other. They went "through the
whole island."

2. Paul's clash with the sorcerer at Paphos was a
typical experience. The early Christians had to meet

and vanquish these men who claimed that by charms and witchcraft they could influence the destiny of men's lives. Although there may have been some portion of good medical knowledge in many a magician's outfit, yet his general methods tended to make men fearful of evil spirits at every turn and any moment. It was no small part of the mission of early Christianity to break the shackles of such superstition by convincing men that the power of the spirit of God in Christ could raise them above every harm from any of these sources. Paul's denunciation checked this sorcerer's career "for a season" and perhaps ended his favor with the proconsul entirely.

3. The impression made upon the proconsul Sergius Paulus was Paul's first victory in a purely Roman situation. The story becomes very real after reading the inscription found on the north coast of Cyprus dated "in the proconsulship of Paulus." Whether that dignified Roman official actually asked to have his name added to the list of church members or not, in any case the incident must have proved a decided encouragement to Paul. His vision of bringing peoples throughout the empire into the fold of the Kingdom received new fuel and new power.

It is probable that the original plan of the tour ended at Paphos. But with this victory kindling his soul Paul could not pause. He must press on to further efforts and further realization of his plan.

4. The fact that Luke here stops calling Paul "Saul" and hereafter uses the name "Paul" is of significance. It is often stated that Paul changed his name at his conversion. If this were true, surely Luke who knew him so

well would have changed the name at that point. Paul
probably had both names from his boyhood. In Tarsus
his Jewish playmates called him Saul and his Roman
playmates called him Paul. Luke, probably following
an Aramaic source, in speaking of him in Palestine and
Syria uses the Jewish name Saul. Up to this point
Paul was to Luke a Jew looking out upon the Roman
world as a possible field for his labors. After the triumph
before the proconsul Paul is a Roman. As a citizen of
the world and of the Roman Empire he now uses the
spirit of Christ which dwells in him as a means of giving
life and light to that great world of which he is a citizen.
From now on in Luke's narrative, and probably also
as a fact of history, Paul forgets that he is Saul, except
when he tells the story of his conversion.

Paul was impatient to proceed. How long he stayed
on the Island of Cyprus, whether the three visited the
home of Barnabas and how long they tarried there,
whether Barnabas' home was in the city, or whether
he came from the country and so was less familiar with
the big cities than Paul—to none of these questions is
there any answer. Luke is true to the newly fired eagerness of Paul in hastening over all details and carrying
his readers away from the island which was the home
of Barnabas to stranger scenes and more difficult experiences. The spirit of Jesus of Nazareth, the spirit of
unbounded and untiring service, has been reincarnated
in Paul the Roman citizen.

3. AT ANTIOCH OF PISIDIA

"Barnabas and Saul" had visited Cyprus. But it
was "Paul and his company" (Acts 13:13) who set sail

from Cyprus.   Luke is very deft in suggesting to us the
rapidly growing leadership of Paul.

Their destination was Perga, the capital of Pamphylia.   This time the voyage was about 175 miles, a
longer one than that from Antioch to Cyprus.   Mark
made the voyage with them but turned back at Perga.
Something must have gone wrong in Perga, for, although
it was an important city and capital, Paul and Barnabas
did not stay long.   There is much to be said in favor of
the explanation that Paul, after his overexertion in
Cyprus and coming into the malarial lowland of the
Pamphylian coast, was taken ill with fever.   This would
account for two things: first, that Paul was displeased
at Mark's desertion, as indicated in Acts 15:39, and,
secondly, that Paul, leaving Perga so suddenly, goes into
the mountains to cities located at an elevation of nearly
4,000 feet.   The best possible antidote for a malarial
attack would be the mountain air.

Like other centers of Paul's activity, Antioch of
Pisidia was a favored place.   The emperor Augustus had
made it a Roman colony.   This meant that its citizens
had special rights, such as personal freedom and im-
munity from certain taxes.   Located at an elevation of
3,600 feet, it overlooked a far-reaching fertile plain to the
southeast.   Its extensive ruins prove its great prominence in the apostolic time.

Drinking in the splendid view of the plain and breathing the rare atmosphere of the mountain, Paul and
Barnabas rode their horses along the highway that led
into the city.   They went to the little inn, or perhaps
they found lodging with some friendly Jew who might
be hoping for a return of the favor when he should some-

time visit Jerusalem. On the first Sabbath, or upon some later Sabbath if Paul's illness at first prevented, they went to the synagogue of the Jews. The order of service was simple. After the call to worship and the prayer came the reading of the Scriptures, first in Hebrew, then in Greek. Then came a talk upon the passages read. If by good fortune there were any present who had come from the mother-community at Jerusalem they would be eagerly invited to give the talk. This was Paul's opportunity.

The first words of Paul's speech were, "Men of Israel and ye that fear God." He was speaking to two classes of hearers. He was addressing the "men of Israel" first. But he had also in mind those others who everywhere attended the synagogues in large numbers, but were unwilling to accept the physical and ceremonial requirements of the Jews. They were the men who "feared God" but were not admitted to the circle of the "men of Israel." They believed in monotheism; they believed that the essence of religion was to "do justly, love mercy, and walk humbly with thy God." These men would naturally welcome Paul's message as a great piece of "good news." Paul's plan was of course to endeavor to convert the Jews and use them in the spread of the gospel. But if he failed to win enough Jews to control the synagogue he knew that with the aid of this outer circle his converts when expelled from the synagogue would find meeting places of their own. Paul had had, perhaps from the day of his conversion, a vision of these men forming, as stated above, a great portal through which the gospel of Jesus would go out into the highways and byways of the nations.

Explaining that Jesus was the long-expected Messiah, Paul rose gradually to the climax of his speech in his assertion that a man is not saved by the law of Moses, but by Christ through faith. Of course Luke did not hear the speech, nor was there anyone present who could take down the speech in shorthand. Nevertheless, since Luke heard later speeches of Paul there is no reason to doubt but that his record has preserved the essential thought. Paul was giving his own experience under law and his vision upon the Damascus road. It must have taken no small amount of courage to stand up in a Jewish synagogue as he did and, by an appeal to the resurrection of Jesus after his condemnation by the Jews, prove that the Jewish national leaders had been vanquished and the old system superseded by a new era of freedom.

His former success before the proconsul Sergius Paulus was now eclipsed by the greater success of this first recorded public address. After the service many gathered around him to inquire further. He was asked to speak again. The next Sabbath, Luke narrates, "almost the whole city" was gathered together to hear him talk of the new freedom in Christ. Never could Paul, after this, doubt the power of his gospel. Neither could the jealous Jews fail to see its strength and the danger with which it threatened their whole legal and ceremonial system.

Paul did not always find organized Jewish opposition to his message. There is no indication that either at Salamis or at Beroea he was forced to leave the synagogue. Many Jews of the Dispersion accepted Paul's message with the same hearty welcome which the people of Galilee had given to Jesus' teaching. Paul's insistence that a man may be saved quite apart from the law was in line with the broader attitude and tendency of the Dispersion. Nevertheless, to many it would appear as a very radical departure from established Jewish custom and point of view. Those Jews who followed closely the leadership of the Pharisees at Jerusalem would naturally in many cases create a very active opposition.

Paul and Barnabas were compelled to leave the synagogue at Antioch and turn to the Gentiles. The Gentiles "were glad." They had the kind of message for which they had been waiting. The news of it spread. The Jews became so alarmed for their time-honored faith that they stirred up a persecution against the new circle of converts and succeeded in expelling Paul and Barnabas from the city. Feeling that their work here was done, they proceeded to the next important city and Jewish center, in order to repeat the same successful program.

4. AT ICONIUM

Traveling along the highroad a distance of about eighty miles, the two apostles reached the city of Iconium. This city had somewhat the same natural advantages as Damascus. A stream from the hills flowing down into a plateau, which because of its elevation was rather dry, gave itself completely to the city and its environs, making it a spot of luxurious fruitfulness. Iconium was a growing city of strategic importance located at a crossroads. It became later, under Hadrian, a Roman colony like Antioch of Pisidia. Under Claudius, and therefore about the time of the visit of Paul and Barnabas, it was honored with the title Claudiconium. It was no exception in Paul's program of planting the gospel in the centers of industrial life.

The apostles hunted up again that simple little edifice, the synagogue of the Jews. Telling again the good news of the Christ who came to welcome all men without respect to class or nationality or legal righteousness into his new brotherhood of love to await his coming, they stirred a multitude both of Jews and of Greeks. Again the Jews saw that their national religious prerogative was threatened. They began to slander Paul and Barnabas and to rouse antipathy against them in the city. Luke is probably true to Paul's spirit when he says that on account of the opposition they "therefore" tarried a long time. It was necessary for them to stay long enough to show by actual test the superiority of the new gospel. Here, as in other cities where Paul preached, a little circle may be pictured in which were realized the principles of Christian fellowship, in which the poor was the brother of the rich, in which each man or woman spoke to his neighbor as to an equal, in which the members felt deeply the indwelling power of the Spirit and awaited expectantly the day when the Kingdom of Christ should be established throughout the world. The circle widened. It began to undermine the influence of the Jewish synagogue and its ceremonial. The thousand enactments of the Mosaic law and the rabbinic explanations of them were losing ground. The Jews succeeded as at Antioch in creating a mob spirit against Paul and Barnabas. But the work of the two was done. They could be of greater service by leaving and going to another city than by staying and increasing the bitter antagonism which had been aroused.

Two little touches in Luke's narrative are among the facts which give us confidence in his general accuracy in describing these incidents. In Acts 14:4 he speaks of Paul and Barnabas as "apostles." This clearly reflects that earlier stage in which the term "apostle" had not yet been copyrighted. The later church, even at the time when the Book of Acts was written, would hardly have called Barnabas an apostle. A second touch is in Acts 14:6. Luke says that after leaving Iconium they came to the cities of Lycaonia. This is a reflection of the fact that although Iconium was also geographically in Lycaonia its people were more Phrygian in character. Luke, or his source, knew the people. He was not merely following a map. When the apostles came to Lystra they were not only in Lycaonia but also among Lycaonians.

5. AT LYSTRA AND DERBE

Lystra was only eighteen miles farther along the road. But it was over 400 feet higher than Iconium. The view became continually more open as the two travelers proceeded until they reached a height of about 3,800 feet. One who has traveled in the mountains cannot fail to think of the rising jubilant spirits of the two as they climbed. Their success had been more than they had hoped. Their vision of the expansion of the Christian religion was perhaps enlarging as rapidly as their natural horizon.

The stream which flows down out of the hills to make a fruitful valley around Lystra has a certain suggestiveness in connection with Paul's arrival. As at Damascus and as at Iconium, the stream never reaches the sea. It loses itself completely in its task of irrigation and fertilization. As Paul looked at that stream flowing along in the sunlight, did he perhaps think of his own glad spirits as they were about to give themselves to this city? Did he think that perhaps he like that stream might never proceed farther, that he might give his very life to the city and be dragged out of it as one who was dead? Surely he did not know what fruit his sacrifice would bear, nor dream that a certain young man from Lystra named Timothy would become his greatest helper, and would after his death be his successor, traveling up and down the Roman Empire strengthening and confirming the churches.

Lystra was a city worthy of Paul's labors. On the present site of the city there still stands in its original place the pedestal of a statue of the emperor Augustus. Possibly this was the site of emperor-worship. A new bit of information was turned up in 1885 in the shape of a coin bearing the significant inscription that Lystra was a Roman colony. In this Roman colony Paul the Roman citizen was to undergo his first serious persecution.

Luke does not record that Paul and Barnabas went to a synagogue. Perhaps the omission only shows Luke's lack of information. Possibly there was no synagogue. But it is also quite possible that the apostles wished to avoid another clash with the Jews, for Lystra was only a short distance from Iconium. Luke gives the impression that here it was not preaching concerning Jewish law and salvation, but the healing of a cripple which attracted the chief attention. It is not hard to understand how Paul may at times, through the force of his own personality and with the aid of the power of faith in Christ, have relieved such cases. Luke's interest seems to have been chiefly in the power exhibited, while for students of the life of Paul the account contains also an instructive suggestion of the personal side of Paul's work. Like Jesus he turned aside at any time to help the poor and the helpless and others whom he found in trouble (cf. I Thess. 2:11; Acts 20:31, 35).

Greek and Roman mythology illustrate abundantly how common was the idea that the gods might at any time visit earth and go about *incognito* mingling in human affairs. Nevertheless, Luke's account indicates that the people of Lystra were profoundly and deeply impressed, that they had never seen two men so filled with the divine spirit as these two. As their enthusiasm and imagination were fired, they could say that Barnabas was Jupiter himself and that Paul was his spokesman, Mercury, the messenger of the gods.

The personal appearance of the two apostles can be interestingly described in view of these appellations. Barnabas was evidently a heavy man with a dignified bearing. His bearded face may be imagined after the pattern of the busts of Jupiter which have found their way into our museums. Paul, on the other hand, like Mercury, the messenger of the gods, was smooth-faced, quick of foot, and quick of eye. He was the spokesman, the active one. The incident is an effective commentary on the slander of Paul's enemies which he quotes in II Cor. 10:10: "His letters they say are weighty and strong, but his bodily presence is weak and his speech of no account." The conclusion should not be too hastily drawn from the Corinthian passage that Paul had an impediment in his speech. Perhaps it was his very eloquence that brought the retort that his impassioned language was "of no account."

The men of Lystra spoke more truly than they knew when they described him as that messenger of the gods with the winged feet. For he combined in a unique and marvelous way the gift of interpreting messages from heaven to earth with that other gift of speeding on the wings of faith and service to the uttermost parts.

At the gateway through which the two gods had come into their city the people prepared a sacrifice in honor of their entrance. The priest came from the Temple of Jupiter. Animals were brought for sacrifice and garlands for festive decoration. This turned their adoration into idolatry. Certain men ran to tell Paul and Barnabas. Perhaps the apostles were holding a meeting of Christians in some home. Whatever they were doing, they left immediately and rushed out to the gate to stop the idolatrous rite.

How can the people of this same city so soon afterward have stoned Paul and dragged him out of the city and left him for dead ? Is it not a reminder of that week in which Jesus celebrated his triumphal entry into Jerusalem amid palm branches and hosannas, and then so soon afterward was led out of the city and crucified ? The fanatical hatred in Lystra as in Jerusalem was stirred up by the narrowness and pride of certain Jews who felt that the prestige of their national religion was threatened.

Arrived in Lystra, those Jews who according to Acts 14:5 had attempted a stoning at Iconium probably began to explain the healing of the cripple exactly as the Jews on one occasion explained a marvelous cure of

Jesus (Matt. 12:24). They would say that, as such a physical misfortune was caused by a demon, only a person in league with the demons could have effected a cure. They would explain the wonder as a sign of an evil power. Since the people were apparently impressed only by the unusual character of the cure, and not touched at all by its beneficent quality, they could easily be carried away into an antipathy commensurate with their former respect.

Being stoned is not a pleasant experience. It creates a very different frame of mind from that in which a man usually eats his breakfast or goes to a college classroom. A modern tourist traveling recently through Samaria, after mounting his horse one morning, was proceeding through the village of Nablus. Suddenly a stone thrown from a considerable distance fell into the road beside him. Before the dust of that stone and the alarm it caused had subsided, another one struck his horse full upon the shank, causing the animal to rear and jump. This was followed by many more, mostly from unseen sources. Fortunately he was wearing a stiff rubber helmet so that his head was safe. But that morning was one never to be forgotten. "Once was I stoned," is his summary of the event. And he hopes the affair will never be repeated. Somewhat the same way it happened to Paul. One day, as he was walking through the street, the stones began to fall about him, then faster and faster, until he fell to the pavement and was carried outside the city, where his friends might later come and find his body and prepare it for burial. His last thoughts in the midst of it all must have been of Stephen and Stephen's vision.

One last parallel to the life of Jesus is found in Acts 14:20. Luke hints that Paul was again imitating his Master in rising victoriously from the grave which his enemies had prepared for him.

If his disciples asked him why he suffered such things for the gospel, his reply was that he was making up that which "was lacking in the sufferings of Christ." To save a world is a large task. It requires a great amount of patient labor and suffering. Paul's passion for saving men was supreme. "Woe is me if I preach not the gospel." The "necessity" led him triumphantly forth from that city to the next important center.

The site of Derbe (modern Zoska) has not yet been excavated. There is very little definite knowledge concerning its history. But that it was an important Roman city is shown by the fact that it was called Claudio-Derbe in the reign of Claudius. The only information which Luke gives of the apostles' work here is that they made many disciples. But a casual reference in Acts 20:4 tells that one of Paul's trusted helpers, Gaius by name, came from this city.

Paul was now near the Cilician Gates and could easily by a short trip have crossed through the Taurus Mountains to his home at Tarsus. But his new work gripped him and held him. He turned back again, away from his home, to revisit those stormy scenes of the last weeks and to make more permanent the little new communities which had started up. As he went he explained to them the truth "that through many tribulations we must enter into the kingdom of God." More than this, he selected certain elderly men who should be his representatives until he should come again on another visit.

After retraversing their route as far as Perga, Paul and Barnabas stopped this time long enough to speak the word in that city. Then, full of news which they wished to tell to their friends in Antioch, they went to the port of Attalia and set sail. Partly, perhaps, because of their eagerness to relate their success at Antioch, partly, perhaps, because they were weary with the long journey, Paul and Barnabas did not revisit the island but kept on directly to Antioch. Arrived in the city they rehearsed at the meetings of the little community the experiences of their journey and portrayed the great new possibilities in the bringing of the Gentiles into the Kingdom.

While this first missionary journey may seem small in comparison with later journeys of Paul, it was a new and epoch-making accomplishment. They had covered over 1,400 miles without steamship and without railroads, and without abundance of money to make their journey comfortable. The length of time occupied by the journey, though very hard to estimate accurately, must have been more than a year, perhaps nearly two years. So it was natural that they "tarried no little time" to recuperate and to refill their purses and to lay plans for new conquests.

SUPPLEMENTARY READING

1. Foakes-Jackson, *Saint Paul*, pp. 85–117.
2. McNeile, A. H., *St. Paul*, pp. 28–39.
3. Wood, C. T., *The Life of Paul*, pp. 46–63.
4. Ramsay, *St. Paul the Traveller*, pp. 70–129.
5. Kent, *Work and Teachings of the Apostles*, pp. 86–90.

6. Gilbert, *Student's Life of Paul*, pp. 69–86.
7. Conybeare and Howson, *Life and Epistles of St. Paul*, chaps. v, vi.
8. Farrar, *Life and Work of St. Paul*, chaps. xix–xxi.
9. *Bible for Home and School*, "Acts," pp. 131–47.
10. McGiffert, *A History of Christianity in the Apostlic Age*, pp. 172–92.
11. Jones, *St. Paul the Orator*, pp. 25–61.
12. Bacon, *The Story of St. Paul*, pp. 97–106.
13. On Antioch, Ramsay, *Cities of St. Paul*, pp. 247–314; on Iconium, pp. 317–82; on Derbe, pp. 385–404; on Lystra, pp. 407–19.

CHAPTER VI

EMANCIPATING THE GOSPEL FROM JEWISH LEGALISM

1. THE JEWISH-CHRISTIAN LEGALISTS

The internationalizing of Christianity was by no means an easy or simple process. To lead the way in the bringing in of the Gentiles, or rather to present the gospel in large terms among the nations of the empire without antagonizing the Jewish Christians, was a delicate and difficult task. The Jews, especially in Palestine, considered themselves separate and different from other peoples. They felt that to eat with the " Gentiles" rendered them ceremonially unclean. While Paul was planning further journeys of evangelization, a party of Jewish Christians was arising which threatened seriously to hamper his work. They had no appreciation of the deeply significant experience through which Paul and Barnabas had gone on their first missionary journey.

The men who roused this opposition were from Paul's point of view more Jewish than Christian. Yet to think of them as not sincere in their Christianity is to underestimate the acuteness of the situation. They were men who lacked the broad outlook which Paul possessed. They looked with alarm upon the possible rapid growth of a church independent of Jewish restrictions. What would become of the synagogues, of the sacred law of Moses? They feared that the vast network of Judaism throughout the empire would begin to disintegrate. The elaborate and splendid Temple at Jerusalem would lose its hold on men's imaginations. There was but one possible and sensible course, they said. Let every Christian be circumcised and thus definitely join the great Jewish religion and become a member of the expanding Jewish-Christian church.

It is not hard to imagine some of the arguments which these Judaizers would use in varying ways and circumstances in their efforts to preserve the integrity of their national religion. In fact it is difficult to see how an uninformed gentile convert in Antioch or even in more distant Lystra or Derbe would be able in Paul's absence to withstand the array of propositions. (1) These Judaizers might say Christ himself was a Jew, was circumcised, kept the law of Moses in all essentials. Anyone who wished to be a "Christian" must live as Christ did. (2) They might claim that the Messiah and the messianic kingdom cannot be understood apart from the Jewish Scriptures. They would point out that these Scriptures command circumcision. They would refer with an air of conclusiveness to God's covenant with Abraham, recorded in Gen. 17:7. "To Abraham were the promises spoken and to his seed" (Gal. 3:16).

(3) They could point forcefully to the fact that the apostles all kept the law, not only that they were all circumcised, but that they continued in their general observance of the ceremonial and of obligations to the Temple at Jerusalem. (4) They asserted that Paul was not a true apostle (cf. Gal. 1:1; I Cor. 9:1; II Cor. 11:13; 12:12), that he had not been with Jesus during his earthly ministry and hence could not have received a commission from him, that Paul's gospel was only a making over of what he had heard from the apostles at Jerusalem. (5) They probably said that Paul was acting inconsistently and dishonestly. He was a circumcised Jew and was on the safe side himself. They perhaps accused him of circumcising his friends, as he later circumcised Timothy, of preaching circumcision when he was among Jews, yet preaching liberty to those who were fond of license. (6) Finally, they could represent that Paul was merely letting down the bars and retailing a kind of "get-rich-quick" way of salvation, doing it for the sake of the glory which he derived from it and incidentally for the sake of the collections which he took up in his churches.

This narrow view which regarded Christianity as merely a new chapter in the history of Judaism contrasted sharply with Paul's conception of the gospel as an international message intended for Jew and Gentile alike. There was evident need that Paul should have a conference with the apostles at Jerusalem and come to a clear understanding with them as to their attitude toward his gentile mission.

This conference at Jerusalem was decidedly the most important and significant Christian meeting of the first

century. If the decision of this council had been different, not only would Paul's work have been greatly
hindered, but he and his followers would have founded
a separate religion. This catastrophe of a split into a
Jewish religion of Jesus on the one side and a Pauline
gentile Christianity on the other was averted by the
forceful way in which Paul handled the situation.

2. PAUL'S ACCOUNT OF THE CONFERENCE

In Galatians Paul gives a rather full and complete
statement of his meeting with the apostles. His account
is first-hand testimony written at most only two or
three years after the event. With his companion
Barnabas he went up to Jerusalem. Titus, an uncir-
cumcised gentile convert, was also with him. At Jerusalem in a private conference with the leading apostles
he explained his gospel. The real question at issue was
the circumcision of Gentiles who would become Christians. There were also present at the conference or in
the background influencing it representatives of the
extreme legalists, "the false brethren privily brought in,"
who had come to do what they could to oppose Paul.
The issue converged upon Titus.

At first the pillar apostles adopted a compromise
attitude. They urged Paul to pacify the legalists by
circumcising Titus. The legalists had perhaps represented that the whole controversy was about this one
man, and that if he were circumcised peace would be
restored. Paul knew that the question was of world-
wide import. He regarded any yielding in the case of
Titus as a jeopardizing of "the truth of the gospel."
Paul probably saw also that the attitude of the apostles

was only one of temporary expediency and that inwardly they were not adverse to the broader view. He stood his ground. He "gave place by way of the subjection (demanded), no, not for an hour."

Paul's determined stand won the day. The apostles yielded. They admitted the justice of his contention that the circumcising of Titus involved the vital point of the controversy. They came squarely over to the side of Paul and Barnabas and entered into an agreement with them whereby these two men should preach the gospel without circumcision among the Gentiles while the Jerusalem apostles preached among the Jews. This division of territory ended any disagreement. The outcome of the conference was a most friendly and formal indorsement of Paul's work. The legalists were completely defeated in their opposition. "James and Cephas and John . . . . gave to me and Barnabas the right hands of fellowship."

It was a turning-point in Paul's career. Even without the approval of the apostles he would have continued his gentile mission. But now he had a definite sanction to which he could refer all questioners. At Jerusalem itself, the center of Judaism, his gospel had been speeded on its mission. Possibly the triumphant vindication contributed its share to the new impetus which soon afterward sent Paul all the way to Europe. But perhaps its greatest historical significance lay in its assurance of the unity of early Christendom. This unity was still further promoted by the plea of the apostles that from Paul's gentile churches a contribution should be sent for the relief of the Jewish-Christian poor at Jerusalem.

3. THE ACTS ACCOUNT OF THE CONFERENCE

An event so central and so far-reaching as the Jerusalem conference naturally received place in the Book of Acts. But that book, written so many years after the event, allows room for many uncertainties. There is even some question as to the chapter in which the conference is to be found, whether in chapter 15, as usually held, or possibly in the account of the relief visit in chapter 11.

Three arguments have been advanced for finding the conference in chapter 11. (1) The relief visit of Acts 11:30 would be, in case Paul really went to Jerusalem, his second visit. According to Gal 2:1, the conference occurred on his second visit. (2) In Gal. 2:10 the request at the conference is to remember the poor, "which very thing I was also zealous to do." This corresponds in a way to the purpose of the relief visit. For in time of famine the poor would be the first to receive help from the Antioch commission. (3) At the conference the apostles "imparted nothing" to Paul (Gal. 2:6). This means, especially in conjunction with Gal. 2:10 ("only"), that they laid no restrictions upon Paul's gospel in gentile fields. Acts, chap. 15, however, speaks of certain requirements drawn up in written form at Jerusalem.

But in Acts, chap. 11, there is no mention of a conference. There is not even a direct statement that Paul reached the city of Jerusalem, though the implication is that he did. The request to remember the poor could be made as well on one visit as another. The restrictions mentioned in Acts, chap. 15, create a difficulty which will be considered. But the difficulty is only increased by placing a Jerusalem conference in chapter 11.

The conference of Gal., chap. 2, is almost certainly to be identified with the one described in Acts, chap. 15. There is fundamental and general agreement in the situation portrayed. Both agree that a council was held at which gentile Christianity was freely recognized. Both agree that the circumcision of gentile converts was declared to be unnecessary. They agree in assuming that Jewish Christians were to keep the Mosaic law afterward as before. The public meeting which is described at length in Acts, chap. 15, is probably implied by contrast in the word "privately" in Gal. 2:2. Both state that Paul's personal program of evangelizing the Gentiles was heartily indorsed. Finally both accounts mention James and Peter as having leading parts in the approval.

Comparing Luke's account with Paul's it becomes apparent that Acts, chap. 15, has several statements not found in Galatians.

1. In Acts 15:2 the Antioch Christians "appointed" that Paul and Barnabas should go up, while in Gal. 2:2 Paul "went up by revelation." Paul's account shows that it was he who took the initiative in proposing the conference and that any action taken by the Antioch church was in the nature of support of his decision to go.

2. Again, Galatians mentions only the private conference and Acts only a public one. It is not hard to conceive that the latter general meeting was held. Paul's real victory was won at his session with the apostles, but both Paul and the apostles would wish to

acquaint the Jerusalem Christians with the new and larger view and to gain their approval of this forward step.

An incidental statement in Acts, chap. 15, occurring in verse 4 and again in verse 12, is suggestive of the probable method by which Paul gained the approval of these Jewish Christians. It was not the method of debate. Possibly the Judaizers would have had the best of an extended argument before a Jerusalem audience. Certainly if the basis of appeal had been Old Testament scripture and early Christian custom the plea for the stricter view would have been almost irresistible. But Paul was not to be drawn into a rabbinical discussion in this public meeting. He began by showing them a new dispensation in God's dealing with the Gentiles. He "rehearsed all things that God had done with them, ... what signs and wonders God had wrought among the Gentiles." He would perhaps point to Titus, whom he had brought with him, as an example of a manly gentile Christian. He would tell of "the fruits of the Spirit" as he has listed them in his letters. He would conclude by painting a vivid picture of the "fearers of God" coming into the Kingdom in great numbers and of the hosts of their gentile comrades behind them. His listeners would, at least momentarily, see a vision as he had seen it, of the gates of the Kingdom flung wide open; would see the peoples of every tongue forsaking their unclean ways and in the name of the Jewish Prince preparing themselves for entrance into God's new commonwealth.

Even after hearing of the success of the gospel among the Gentiles the Jerusalem Christians probably took little active interest in the wider program. Paul attained the object of his visit. But the contrast between his intense consecration to the cause of Christ among the nations and their attitude of toleration still remained. The height to which the average Christian in Jerusalem reached is perhaps well expressed in that beautifully negative decision of Acts 15:19, that "we trouble not them that from among the Gentiles turn to God."

3. In Acts 15:23–29 are the so-called decrees of the council contained in an epistle which, Luke narrates, was sent at this time from Jerusalem to Antioch. The four restrictions were apparently to be imposed upon gentile converts, not only in "Antioch and Syria and Cilicia," as stated in the epistle (15:23), but in all Paul's churches generally (cf. 16:4). The chief difficulty with these decrees is the definite statement in Galatians that the apostles "imparted nothing" to Paul, asking "only" that he remember the poor. The whole impression of Paul's account is that the only question at issue in the conference was circumcision, and that here he won a clean victory. Even Acts seems at first to suggest such an outcome, "that we trouble not them that from among the Gentiles turn to God." Moreover, in all Paul's letters there is no trace of any such compromise as the decrees suggest. On the contrary, when the question of eating "things sacrificed to idols" (Acts 15:29; I Cor. 8:1) arose in the Corinthian church Paul wrote plainly, "food will not commend us to God" (I Cor. 8:8). It is hard to conceive that Paul would ever have consented to the imposing of the four requirements, or have been, even in a negative way, a party to any such arrangement.

The Peter incident, also, which took place soon afterward at Antioch (Gal. 2:11 ff.), seems to exclude the possibility that the Jerusalem conference had at that time issued any such decrees.

It is not difficult to account for the presence of the restrictions in Acts. The key to the explanation may be found in the statement that the communication to Antioch was in writing. It is the only case in Acts in which Luke states that he is quoting a Christian document. Perhaps Luke had seen some such missive, or more probably had indirect information that there existed at Antioch such an epistle. In seeking the most likely place for it in his account he not unnaturally decided it belonged to this famous council. Its more probable origin, which is revealed by a study of the document itself, can be best understood after a review of the Peter incident at Antioch.

4. PETER'S VISIT TO ANTIOCH

Paul had been successful in accomplishing his purpose at Jerusalem. His mission to the Gentiles of the empire had been approved. The division of the field into two parts, a Jewish and a gentile, promised to end all disputes. The Jerusalem apostles were to preach among the Jews. Paul was to preach his more liberal presentation of the gospel among the Gentiles. Paul of Tarsus in Cilicia had gone up to Jerusalem, and from those whom he had been accustomed to respectfully regard as the "pillars" he had won the right hand of fellowship.

But there were several important questions upon which the conference had given no decisions. It was natural that in controversy over the main issue other related questions should be left untouched. In general the clear implication of the conference was that in Jewish territory the pillar apostles would continue to win men to faith in Christ without disturbing their relation to the law, and that in gentile territory Paul would win them without imposing circumcision. But were Gentiles in Jewish territory to keep the law if they became Christians? Were Gentiles in gentile territory to keep the law in other matters than circumcision, or were they to be free from other statutes as well? Were Jewish Christians in gentile territory to keep the law? Of course, with them the question of circumcision could not arise personally. But were they to circumcise their children? Would they keep the Sabbath and observe the law of foods? Apparently none of these points was discussed.

One question became particularly urgent. The question of the observance of the Jewish food law in a mixed Christian church was not settled at the conference and apparently had not been raised at all. Paul would doubtless assume that that had been left to him to take care of under the general agreement that gentile lands were his diocese. The extreme legalists would naturally assume that Jews everywhere would continue to keep the law in all respects. The decision of the council presupposed logically both that the law was permanent and that it was not permanent, according to the locality and persons concerned.

After his return from Jerusalem to Antioch Paul began to preach to this gentile territory his gospel of freedom. So effectively did he portray the brotherhood of man with man that Jews and Gentiles formed the habit of eating together, Jews at gentile meals as well as Gentiles at Jewish. Thus Jews were violating the Jewish feeling that eating at a gentile table rendered a Jew unclean.

When Peter came down to Antioch he at first accepted the practice as he found it. For him the logic of the situation was clear. According to the Jerusalem conference the law of circumcision was not binding on gentile Christians. In that case the law was not infallibly binding as law upon Gentiles, and therefore the rest of the statutes were not necessarily binding on Gentiles. But if the statutes were not binding upon Gentiles, neither could they be intrinsically binding upon Jews. Therefore the whole matter was one of expediency. But, in a mere matter of expediency, when the unity of the church becomes involved, Jews should not sacrifice their brotherly unity to observance of the law, and hence they should give up their legal scruples.

Peter perhaps did not consciously argue the matter with himself in any such thoroughgoing way. Feeling may have had more to do with it than thought. He was the same generous, impulsive Peter whom Jesus loved so deeply and rebuked so often. Since Peter's experience with Cornelius he had become more and more convinced of the acceptability of the Gentiles in God's sight. At Antioch he was swept along by the breath of the new atmosphere of freedom in Christ. Jesus had eaten with publicans and sinners. Why should his apostles hesitate to eat with Gentiles? He little dreamed what a controversy he would stir up by eating with some of the new Christian friends. He was simply conscious in a general way that the Jerusalem agreement left gentile territory under the direction of Paul and Barnabas, and hence that in Antioch he was free to follow Antioch customs. From Paul's point of view he was right.

Then came the brethren from James, the head of the Jerusalem church. Possibly the same extreme legalists who were present at the conference had induced James to send a delegation to see just how matters stood in Antioch. When they arrived they protested against Peter's conduct. The ground of their protest is not difficult to see. They also stood on the Jerusalem compact, which they interpreted to mean only that Gentiles were not to be circumcised. There was no suggestion at the conference that Jewish Christians were to be free from the obligations of the law. In other words, it was the incompleteness and logical inconsistency of the Jerusalem agreement which was the real cause of the whole embarrassing situation. The essentially compromise character of that treaty furnished easy ground for contrary inferences which were actually put into effect by both sides.

What would Peter do? In earlier years he had followed Jesus courageously, until one day at Caesarea Philippi he had voiced the hesitating, fearsome attitude of the disciples. Again he had followed even to the shadow of the cross and there had been drawn away into a triple denial of his leader. At Antioch too he probably began to think of unpleasant consequences not only for himself but for Jewish Christians generally. He would reason that the Jews especially in Palestine were very strict in their observance of the law. They regarded it as the word of God for every son of Abraham. It was

God's covenant with his chosen people. If he, Peter, should become careless about observing this law, not only would he offend his fellow Jewish Christians, but he would be entirely shut away from the unconverted Jews to whom he expected to devote his life. His whole program of Christian mission among the circumcision would be destroyed.

Peter yielded. He carried with him all the Jews, including even Barnabas, Paul's fellow-worker and fellow-traveler. The extreme legalist interpretation of the Jerusalem compact, which excluded any inferences from it as to the law of foods or the freedom of the Jews from law, was on the point of prevailing. This made the situation very unpleasant for the Gentiles, compelling them to choose between a division of the church and subjection on their part to the whole law, including perhaps eventually the rite of circumcision. This pressure upon the Gentiles Paul describes in Gal. 2:14 as an "attempt to compel them to Judaize."

It was another real crisis in Paul's battle for the freedom of the gospel. Paul's sense of injustice was aggravated by Peter's inconsistency. Peter had indicated by his eating with the Gentiles that he believed in Christian liberty. By withdrawing he seemed to show that he could allow his outward conduct to differ from his inward conviction. The vigorous way in which Paul gripped and handled the situation is not unlike some of his later powerful strokes in meeting crises in Galatia and in Corinth.

The sharp rebuke which he addressed to Peter was given added weight and poignancy by the fact that it was a public one "before them all." Those words of

Jesus at Caesarea Philippi, "Get thee behind me, Satan," were intense, but in a measure they were privately spoken. Paul's words, too, were intense. They were double-edged. "If thou being a Jew livest as do the Gentiles . . . . how compellest thou the Gentiles to live as do the Jews?" And the fact that the rebuke was public certainly had its effect upon Peter and upon the whole audience. How complete Paul's success was is not told. Probably the result was to bring the whole church back to Paul's viewpoint. In favor of this view is the statement of Acts 18:22, 23, that Paul returned and spent some time here after his next missionary journey.

Incidentally the study of the Antioch crisis makes it possible to understand the probable origin of the document of Acts, chap. 15, containing the "decrees." For centuries, especially since the conquests of Alexander the Great, the Jews of Jerusalem and of Palestine had been confronted with the problem of association with men of other nations who wished to live in Palestine. To meet the situation a list of "seven Noachian prohibitions" was drawn up. Jews might associate with any Gentile who observed these seven restrictions. There is a difference of opinion as to whether the seven were primarily moral or ceremonial. Hence there is also question as to whether the prohibitions in Acts coincide with three or possibly with four of the Noachian. But the general connection of the two lists is clear.

There probably arose, then, in Palestine among early Christians this same question. How far could Jewish Christians associate with gentile Christians and still be known as good Jews? Apparently the apostles in an effort to conciliate the extreme legalists reached a compromise decision that among Jewish Christians three or four of the seven restrictions would be placed upon the gentile believer, not as a basis of Christian standing, but as a basis of association with Jews. His faith in Christ would be considered as a just equivalent for obedience to the omitted prohibitions. Thus association together in one church would be possible. Just when this question arose and this decision was reached is uncertain. Paul would not naturally be concerned with it or be in sympathy with any other than a very local application of it. It is, however, quite possible that at some time there was an attempt to extend its validity as far as Antioch in order to avoid recurrence of such unpleasant scenes as Paul's public rebuke of Peter.

The general effect upon Paul of the Peter incident and of later related controversies was to drive him to very clear statements of his position regarding the Jewish law and the freedom of the gospel. The early Jewish-Christian ideal seems to have been to admit certain Gentiles generously into the fold and possibly in certain ways to associate with them as Jesus had associated with the "publicans and sinners." In contrast to this Paul took the radical stand upheld in Gal. 2:16, 19; 3:23, 24; II Cor. 3:6, and many other passages that the Mosaic law is utterly worthless as a direct means of making a man acceptable to God. The gospel of freedom is the only true gospel. Jesus had told his disciples that the spirit was above the letter of the law, that the letter might be broken on occasion if it conflicted with the higher law, "Thou shalt love thy neighbor as thyself." Paul took the position that the law had in Christ been entirely done away. It was meant for children, keeping them in ward till Christ should come (Gal. 3:23). The man who is in Christ is full grown. In fact the keeping of the law has a blinding and deadening effect which is quite out of line with the free exercise of the spirit of love in Christ.

In looking back over the course of Paul's battle for the emancipation of the gospel from Jewish legalism it is possible to distinguish three stages of advance.

1. At Jerusalem, Paul was successful in establishing the principle that the gospel may be preached to the Gentiles without laying upon them any pressure to become Jews by rite of circumcision.

2. At Antioch, before the arrival of delegates from Jerusalem, Paul won such a recognition of Christian brotherhood as permitted fraternal association between Jewish Christians and gentile Christians. The conference at Jerusalem which sanctioned Paul's gospel for gentile territory was quite properly interpreted as approving complete fellowship in a gentile church. So successful was Paul in presenting and fostering this liberal point of view that not only Barnabas but Peter himself fell in with this new custom.

3. Peter's withdrawal, carrying back all the Jews, even Barnabas included, showed Paul the fundamental narrowness of the Jewish attitude. Paul advanced to that third and lofty vantage ground from which he never retreated. The whole Jewish law is of no use whatsoever as a way of winning favor with God. Christ is all-sufficient. The gospel was intended directly for the world. The Jewish-Christian attitude that Gentiles may be received into the Jewish Kingdom Paul

completely reversed. He invited Jews to join that world-kingdom in which the only law is the spirit of Christ. The letter killeth, but the spirit giveth life.

SUPPLEMENTARY READING

1. Foakes-Jackson, *Saint Paul*, pp. 118–27.
2. McNeile, A. H., *St. Paul*, pp. 40–50.
3. Wood, C. T., *Life of Paul*, pp. 92–97.
4. Ramsay, *St. Paul the Traveller*, pp. 152–77.
5. Kent, *Work and Teachings of the Apostles*, pp. 94–99.
6. Gilbert, *Student's Life of Paul*, pp. 87–106.
7. Conybeare and Howson, *Life and Epistles of St. Paul*, chap. vii.
8. Farrar, *Life and Work of St. Paul*, chaps, xxii–xxiii.
9. *Bible for Home and School*, "Acts," pp. 147–54.
10. McGiffert, *A History of Christianity in the Apostolic Age*, pp. 192–217.
11. Bacon, *The Story of St. Paul*, pp. 107–46.
12. Cone, *Paul*, pp. 69–94.

CHAPTER VII

"COME OVER INTO MACEDONIA"

1. REVISITING THE CHURCHES

After the stormy events at Jerusalem and at Antioch Paul naturally became anxious about the welfare of the churches which he and Barnabas had founded. As he had now become the leading spirit, it was he who proposed to Barnabas that they revisit their new "brothers" and see "how they fare." The disagreement which ensued between them must have been very unpleasant for both.

Paul remembered how Mark had forsaken them in the middle of the first journey. He felt that the task of establishing the gospel throughout the Roman Empire needed such resolute courage as Jesus had in mind when he said, "No man having put his hand to the plow and looking back is fit for the kingdom of God" (Luke 9:62). But Mark was Barnabas' own cousin, and Barnabas was determined to give him another chance. So the separation came. Paul's attitude doubtless proved a strong

incentive to Mark to make himself worthy of Barnabas'
confidence. In any case Mark's influence was a growing
one, even down to the day when he wrote what is our
earliest extant life of Christ.

It is also possible that Paul's plans for the journey
were too ambitious for Barnabas. They may have
seemed visionary and impracticable. The act of Barnabas in siding with Peter (Gal. 2:11) may also have
disturbed the formerly close friendship. Perhaps, too,
there was a difference in regard to the route which they
should take, Paul desiring to visit his own home first
and the cities of Asia Minor, while Barnabas wished first
to visit his own home in Cyprus and the disciples there.

Although Paul and Barnabas were "men of like
passions" with others, as they told the crowd at Lystra,
they did not part as enemies. They acted in a logical
and Christian way. They divided the churches into
two groups, Barnabas setting sail from the Seleucia pier
for Cyprus, Paul accepting responsibility for the churches
of the mainland. The work on the island must have
flourished, for Cyprus afterward became prominent in
early Christian history. Meanwhile Paul, looking about
for a suitable companion, chose Silas, whose work and
character he had been observing for some time.

Setting out from Antioch by the land route, Paul and
Silas on their first day's journey traveled along the pic-
turesque road up through the Syrian Gates in the little
range of hills which every tourist must cross today in
riding from Antioch to the modern port at Alexandretta.
As the path then led them out of sight of the city of
Antioch, Paul and Silas would be talking together, not
only of revisiting churches already founded, but of

carrying the news to far more distant countries. After following the shore for a few miles they came to Issus. Probably they slept there the first night, within sound of the waves of the Mediterranean. Paul would remember the history of the city as clearly as any American remembers the story of Bunker Hill or Lexington. He knew that the battle which Alexander had here fought decided that the culture of Macedonia should penetrate Syria and Palestine. Perhaps he resolved that night in some dim way that the new religion of Palestine, going in the reverse direction, should penetrate if possible even to Macedonia. We have already noted the interesting coincidence that Paul journeyed with the power of the gospel through Asia Minor and over into Macedonia by practically the same route which Alexander had traversed with his phalanxes on his eastward march.

At the end of a second or perhaps a third day the riders would reach Tarsus. Paul would be glad to see his home again even if only for a few days. Perhaps there was a Christian church there, for Acts 15:41 speaks of "confirming the churches of Syria and Cilicia." But the tone of Luke's narrative harmonizes, as it frequently does, with Paul's desire to proceed rapidly. We hear nothing of his greeting former friends, nothing of his family, nothing of the fruits of the gospel in his own city, for Paul's thoughts were on more distant scenes.

Leaving Tarsus he crossed the Taurus Mountains by the Cilician Gates through which Alexander had come, and through which Cyrus had marched with his 10,000 Greeks. Four long days of travel brought him to familiar localities at Derbe. Again we have no details concerning his meeting with his Christian friends, his answers to their inquiries about Barnabas, his introducing of Silas, nor any account of the effect of news concerning the council.

At Lystra Paul found the helper who should fill the place of Mark, as Silas had filled the place of Barnabas. Timothy and his mother had apparently been converted on the apostle's first visit. And when on his first journey he had retraced his steps to the same town he had probably given Timothy especial work to do. For when Paul now for the third time came to Lystra he found Timothy well reported of not only at Lystra, but at Iconium, eighteen miles away.

Paul has been much criticized for circumcising Timothy. This yielding to Jewish legalism, especially after the Jerusalem council at which Paul had stood his ground in regard to Titus, does seem strange. But Paul felt that neither circumcision availeth anything "nor uncircumcision" (Gal. 5:6). His attitude indicates a dominating elevation of soul which was far above insistence upon uniformity in any matter of ceremonial. The all-important consideration was the publishing of the gospel to the world. To this end Paul had his definite policy of approaching the Jews first in each city to which he came. It was the natural and logical way. Unless he were to shut himself out from the company of those who were of primary instrumental importance in his enterprise, his immediate helpers must be Jews.

After visiting Derbe and Lystra "they went through the region of Phrygia and Galatia, having been forbidden of the Holy Spirit to speak the word in Asia" (Acts 16:6). A usual view of this verse has been that Paul in his onward journey from Lystra, reaching the border of the province of Asia, was turned northward through Phrygia; that after traversing Phrygia he came to the region of Galatia, so named after the Gauls who had migrated from Europe; that he here founded churches in various cities, perhaps including Ancyra; and that it was to these churches that he afterward addressed the letter "to the Galatians." This view is now known as North Galatian.

A difficulty with this view is the absence of any statement that Paul founded a series of new churches. The impression of the narrative is that Paul was hastening through toward Macedonia, passing by the intermediate possibilities in Asia, in Bithynia, and in Mysia. Another objection is that the phrase "region of Phrygia and Galatia"[1] naturally means not two regions but one region, which was both Phrygian and Galatic. Still another factor is the statement in the letter to the Galatians (4:13) that it was because of illness that he first preached the gospel to them. The climate and general conditions of the northern district hardly adapted it to be a retreat for an invalid.

The South Galatian view takes as its starting-point the fact that the Roman province of Galatia included not only the northern ethnic Galatia, but also several other small states, and in particular included, in its southern part, Derbe, Lystra, Iconium, Antioch. Galatia is used in this larger sense in I Pet. 1:1. In this province of Galatia one part was Phrygian. Luke's phrase may refer, then, to the district which is both Phrygian and Galatian, viz., the Phrygian portion of the province of Galatia. Only a part of Phrygia was

[1] τὴν Φρυγίαν καὶ Γαλατικὴν χώραν.

incorporated in Galatia. There was also a Phrygia of Asia. Hence the necessity of the double designation, "the region of Phrygia and Galatia."

In Luke's geography Galatian Phrygia included Iconium and Antioch. Derbe and Lystra were in Lycaonia. Cicero speaks of Iconium as Lycaonian, but Xenophon refers to it as Phrygian. Acts 14:6 shows that Luke did not think of it as Lycaonian. For him it was over the line in Phrygia.

The South Galatian view, then, holds that Paul after visiting Derbe and Lystra (16:1) went through the Phrygian Galatian region, in particular through Iconium and Antioch. He was not expecting at first to go in this direction as far as Antioch, but was going to join the main highroad, which entered Asia at a point considerably east of Antioch. A glance at the map will show that from Iconium it is three times as far to Antioch as to the nearest point of Asia. But "having been forbidden of the Holy Spirit" he did not yet enter Asia, but stayed in the province of Galatia, journeying through the region of Phrygia in Galatia.

On this view, since Paul did not visit ethnic Galatia at all, the letter to the Galatians was addressed to the churches of the first missionary journey, Derbe, Lystra, Iconium, Antioch. He refers to his readers as "Galatians" (3:1), not only because as a Roman citizen he was accustomed to use Roman designations, but also because it was the only common term by which he could collectively address both Lycaonians and Phrygians. The illness of which he writes (4:13) was probably, as stated before in connection with the first journey, a malarial fever contracted on the coast, for which the altitudes of the South Galatian cities, averaging over 3,500 feet, would be exceedingly beneficial. And the repeated references to Barnabas which he makes in the epistle (cf. especially 2:9, 13) were allusions to the apostle with whom they became so well acquainted on that first missionary journey.

In any case as Paul journeyed he was guided by the Spirit of Jesus westward and northward. Just what form this guidance assumed is not stated. Perhaps Paul met obstacles through which the Spirit spoke. This is suggested by the words "forbidden" and "suffered not." Yet it is quite as possible that Paul had within him some vision of distant conquest through which the Spirit called and led. When he essayed to go into Bithynia the Spirit again told him this was not his goal. Perhaps along with the impulse to go yet farther was some dim idea of reaching a point where Jewish opposition would not be as violent as in some cases on the first journey—some large and important city where there was no synagogue to arouse organized opposition. Certainly it is interesting to look forward and to note that at Philippi there was no synagogue and that the Philippian Christians later constituted his most loyal church.

2. AT PHILIPPI

The Spirit of Jesus directed Paul onward as far as Troas on the coast. Even here he did not pause. He saw in a vision a man of Macedonia beseeching him, "Come over and help us." A psychological occasion of this vision is perhaps suggested by the sudden introduction of the pronoun "we" in Acts 16:10. It is the first time that the pronoun has occurred in this way in the

Book of Acts. A further study of these "we" sections
makes it seem probable that the author of the narrative
joined Paul at this point and continued with him to
Philippi and helped in the work there. The use of the
pronoun ceases at Philippi after Acts 16:17 as abruptly
as it began. In 20:5 the pronoun reappears again at
Philippi on the third journey. The author was then
perhaps a man of Philippi, who, being in Troas on other
business or having come there for that purpose, had
invited Paul to go to Macedonia to preach the gospel.
This invitation as Paul pondered on it prepared the way
for the vision which decided him to go.

The greatness of Paul's plans at this time and always
forbids us to see in the man of Macedonia merely the
individual Luke, even if the vision-man had his features.
The great importance Paul attached to his vision suggests rather that whoever the individual seemed to be
he was essentially the incarnation of the needs of Macedonia for the gospel story.

It may be remarked in passing that these "we"
sections (16:10–17; 20:5–15; 21:1–18; 27:1—28:16)
were evidently copied out of a diary which Luke kept
at the time of the incidents recorded and constitute a
first-hand historical source of great value (cf. p. 2).

Having now a definite piece of work before them the
four comrades set sail from Troas. Disembarking at
Neapolis, they proceeded nine miles inland to Philippi.
This city was larger and more important than any of the
cities of the first missionary journey. It was Paul's
first stopping-place on this second journey. Each
important center of Paul's activity was larger than any
of the preceding. Their historical order on Paul's

journeys was the order of climax. Thessalonica was
more important than Philippi, and Corinth greater than
either. Ephesus, where he labored three years on his
third missionary journey, was greater than any city
visited on his previous journeys. Rome was the last
and greatest of all.

Philippi was a Roman colony. Luke notes the fact
with some pride. Brutus and Cassius after their assas-
sination of Julius Caesar fled toward the east. At
Philippi in 42 B.C. they were defeated in battle by
Anthony and the young Octavius, afterward the emperor
Augustus. It was in honor of this occasion that Augus-
tus made the city a colony, giving it a government like
that of Rome itself and declaring all its citizens to be
Roman citizens. It was as though a piece of the city of
Rome had been transferred to this spot.

Luke also calls it the first city of the district, a
designation which is hardly correct, since Amphipolis in
the same district ranked ahead of it. The little statement reminds us forcefully that we are reading Luke's
estimate of his own native city. In his opinion it was
the first city. It is not at all likely that Luke's statement should be understood as meaning that Philippi
was the first Roman "colony" of the district. Luke was
thinking of his city's history and influence and possibilities. It is the only city which he favors with such
special description.

While there was no synagogue at Philippi, there were
Jews there who on the Sabbath met at an appointed
place of prayer outside the city. They chose a spot
near the river, perhaps for the sake of their ceremonial
washings. Luke had probably often visited the spot.

He was certainly one of those devout Greeks who feared God.

Lydia was a native of the Lydian city of Thyatira, one of the seven cities of Asia Minor to which the letters in the Book of Revelation were afterward addressed. She was a woman of some means who had opened a store or bazaar in Philippi. Paul's gospel of the new life of fraternity in mystic communion with the risen Jesus made a strong appeal to her. She not only came out openly on the side of the new gospel, but she did the apostles a much-needed and much-appreciated service by offering her home as a meeting-place. Her house was probably larger than Luke's. This would explain why the apostles preferred to take up their abode there.

Luke's diary, then, opened with this story of a woman's part in the service of the Kingdom. The second incident, too, is about a woman. Luke in his two books, the Gospel and the Acts, has preserved more narratives about women in their relation to Christianity than all the rest of the New Testament writers put together. Paul, too, often mentions the names of women in his churches. Two at Philippi are named in Phil. 4:2. In Gal. 3:28 Paul says there is no distinction in the gospel between male and female. The whole early Christian attitude was in marked contrast to the prayer in the Jewish liturgy in which the worshipers offer thanks that they were not born women.

In the second incident of Luke's diary he narrates that the evangelists made the acquaintance of "a certain maid who had a spirit of divination." The expression was a common one, indicating that the girl practiced

ventriloquism.   The art was popularly so little understood that the peculiar voice of the ventriloquist passed
for the voice of a spirit.   This girl, who took in "much
money" for her masters, apparently had a fairly good
mind.   It is not unlikely that she was very unhappy in
her life of subjection and slavery.   The preaching of
Paul and his companions concerning the freedom that
is in Christ appealed to her as soon as she heard it.   She
cried out after them that they were true men of God.   But
she could not break with her profession and her masters,
until one day after several such scenes Paul turned to
her and in the name of Jesus released her mind from its
bondage.

When her masters saw that the hope of their gain
was gone they set out to prosecute Paul and Silas and
dragged them into court.   How deeply the following
events impressed Paul with a sense of injustice is shown
by a later reference in a letter to Thessalonica, his next
stopping-place.   In I Thess. 2:2 he writes of "having
suffered before and been shamefully treated as ye know
at Philippi."   The masters of the girl were angered, not
only at being robbed of the girl's services, but probably
also by the fear that their other slaves would be similarly
reformed.   They took advantage of that race prejudice
against the Jews which was present everywhere in the
empire.   This was the very year in which Claudius
expelled the Jews from Rome (Acts 18:2).   They
succeeded in bringing a crowd into the court which made
a demonstration.   The easy-going Roman officials felt
that the best solution of the situation was to have the
apostles publicly punished and then put out of sight
into jail.   This must have been one of the three

instances of being "beaten with rods" which Paul mentions in II Cor. 11:25.

Paul and Silas, thrown into prison, immediately began telling the "good news" to their fellow-prisoners. As these listened to Paul's description of his former life of bondage and darkness and guilt and to the strongly contrasted portrayal of his later Damascus experience of liberty and light and justification, they would forget the fetters and the darkness and the prison walls. The place would be filled with praying and singing.

Meanwhile Timothy and Luke had not been idle. We may suppose that they had insistently demanded an interview with the magistrates. The information that Paul and Silas were Roman citizens must certainly have come as a shock to these officials. In view of their offense, even though it were unwitting, they might well tremble for their official position in such a case as this. At about the same time the earthquake shook the foundations of the prison and opened its doors for Paul and Silas. Earthquakes were not uncommon in Mediterranean lands. When the officials sent word to have the apostles set free, the messengers reported not only that prisoners, and jailer too, had been converted, but that the apostles demanded as a reparation for their injustice that the officials come in person and escort them from the prison. It is possible that Paul and Silas made this demand, not merely to vindicate themselves before their fellow-prisoners, but also to protect the converted jailer; for the magistrates, learning of his conversion, might later have blamed the jailer for the escape of the apostles and have deprived him of his position.

The papyrus sheets from the first century give us several glimpses into the prison life of the day and into the hopeless spirit of most victims. The influence which Paul and Silas had over their fellow-prisoners stands out in sharp contrast to the usual whining and complaining (cf. Flinders Petrie, *Pap*. III, 35, 36).

When Paul and Silas left the prison they went back to the house of Lydia. After conferring with the company of disciples they decided to follow the request of the officials and leave the city. It was not Paul's plan to win whole cities to righteousness. The gospel was rather to be planted in the great centers, as seed is quietly sown in selected ground.

Later references show how well Paul had planted at Philippi. In his letter to the Philippians there is more affectionate regard and more appreciation of service rendered than in any other letter of the New Testament. Here arose Paul's most loyal church. The Philippians sent money to assist him in his work in Thessalonica, and then sent a second time to Thessalonica, as mentioned in Phil. 4:16. Later they sent aid during Paul's stay in Corinth, as he relates with feeling in II Cor. 11:9. Finally when he was in prison they overwhelmed him with an especially bountiful gift, for which he can hardly find adequate words of appreciation (Phil. 4:18).

3. AT THESSALONICA

Amphipolis and Apollonia were cities of considerable size. In passing through both without stopping Paul showed his impatience to reach the very center of Macedonian life. Thessalonica, about ninety miles from Philippi, had recently, in 44 A.D., become the home of the governor and government of the whole province of Macedonia. The strategic importance of "Saloniki" has been vividly shown in modern times in the military reports of the world-war. The city had had a great history. It was mentioned frequently by Herodotus and Thucydides under the name "Thermae." Xerxes stopped here on his march into Greece. In 315 B.C. it was rebuilt by Cassander and named Thessalonica, after the sister of Alexander the Great. Cicero spent some time here in exile. Rome allowed it to have its own government, making it a "free city." The appearance of the city as seen from the sea was a striking one. Like Genoa, it was built in the shape of a great amphitheater looking out upon the gulf.

Concerning the beginning of the gospel in Thessalonica Paul himself gives a long description and much detailed information in I Thessalonians. He says in 1:9 concerning "what manner of entering in we had unto you," that they "turned from idols." This shows that most of the Thessalonian Christians had been Gentiles rather than Jews or "devout Greeks"; for these were not worshipers of idols. The Jewish element in the church was so small that he could thus practically ignore it in writing his letter.

As Paul continues his recital in I Thessalonians he draws a contrast (2:1 f.) between his shameful treatment at Philippi and his cordial welcome and the large response to his message at Thessalonica. Their faith had not been shaken even when severe persecution and affliction ensued (1:6; 2:14). Paul indicates further that his stay in Thessalonica was of considerable duration, some months at the least, for he refers at length to his manner

of life among them. Then, too, although he worked
"night and day," he stayed long enough to want the
assistance of the Philippian Christians who, hearing of
his need, sent to his aid, and again later hearing of his
situation sent help a second time (Phil. 4:16). This
prolonged ministry had its personal as well as its public
side. "We dealt with each one of you as a father with
his own children" (2:11). "Ye were become very dear
to us" (2:8).

Paul's words thus reflect a successful work of several
months at Thessalonica, chiefly among the Gentiles.
The incompleteness of Luke's narrative in Acts is at
once apparent. With only his narrative we should
suppose that Paul did not remain long after the "three
sabbath days" of Acts 17:2. Again, although Luke
speaks of a "great multitude" of the "devout Greeks,"
he does not narrate any departure from the synagogue
with consequent turning to the Gentiles. After describing the first three weeks he turns immediately to the
events connected with Paul's departure. The incompleteness of his narrative at this point is in sharp contrast with the accuracy and fulness of the "we" sections
in which he is telling what he himself witnessed and
shared in. In one respect, however, he is notably
accurate. He refers to the magistrates of Thessalonica
as "politarchs," a title found nowhere else in literature,
though abundantly attested by inscriptions.

The Jews "being moved with jealousy" and with a
genuine concern for the prestige of their great Jewish
religion, stirred up a mob. The law of Rome demanded
toleration of religious beliefs. Hence the accusation
against the newcomers was not a religious but a political

one. The charge was that, in preaching a spiritual kingdom of brotherhood to appear in the near future, they were in reality anarchists in that they were unsettling people's minds toward the Roman government. Paul and Silas remembering their experience at Philippi decided not to face the crowd, but laid plans to make their departure quietly.

When the excited people stormed the house where the travelers had been stopping, they had to content themselves with arresting Jason. Just as Lydia, in whose house the converts met in Philippi, was a woman of some means, so Jason appears to have had considerable influence. When he was accused of harboring revolutionists who claimed that there was "another king" (Acts 17:7), he was released as soon as he had given bonds. Probably Jason's bond was taken as a surety that Paul and Silas would leave the city. Not wishing to give Jason further trouble they "immediately" left that same "night."

They had "planted" the seed. It seems to have sprouted and grown more rapidly for a while than at Philippi. It was only a few months later that Paul wrote in I Thess. 2:1 that his ministry had "not been found vain." In 2:14 of the same letter he makes grateful reference to their endurance of persecutions, likening these to the sufferings of the first Christians in Judea. In 4:9, 10, and especially in 1:7, 8, he speaks of their progress in the gospel in no ordinary terms: "Ye became an example to all that believed in Macedonia and in Achaia. . . . . In every place your faith to God-ward is gone forth." In Acts 20:4 we read that two of the Thessalonians traveled with Paul in his company for a while, and in Acts 27:2 that one of these embarked with Paul from Palestine on the voyage to Rome.

<h3>4. AT BEROEA</h3>

Arrived at Beroea Paul found the Jews more hospitable than at any place thus far visited. They received the word with all readiness. Their attitude must have been a joy to Paul. If he was endeavoring to travel far enough from Jerusalem to find Jews who were free from the narrow ceremonial view, he was not to be disappointed. He was right in anticipating that the more broad-minded, cosmopolitan Jews of the empire would welcome his message and see its truth. Hereafter, except for the visit of the Jews from Thessalonica, Paul experienced no serious opposition from the Dispersion. Even at Corinth the hostility of a few did not amount to persecution until after Paul had preached there a year and a half, and then resulted in a signal victory for him.

In Macedonia the only Jews who persecuted Paul were those of Thessalonica. Encouraged by their previous success they now came to Beroea, where they stirred up considerable antagonism. As at Thessalonica, so here their accusations were probably to the effect that Paul was prophesying the coming of "another king" and another kingdom. Paul's friends fearing for his safety escorted him out of the city. Silas and Timothy were able to stay and encourage the new disciples.

Paul's stay in Beroea probably lasted several weeks. "Not a few" joined the new faith. As Luke told of women converts at Philippi, so also at Thessalonica (17:4), at Beroea (17:12), and at Athens (17:34), he tells of the women who helped in the gospel. The church at Beroea, planted by Paul and nurtured for a time by Silas and Timothy and other helpers, became a prosperous one. For it contributed some years later to the collection which Paul took up for the Jerusalem community. One of its members who accompanied Paul is mentioned in Acts 20:4.

SUPPLEMENTARY READING

1. Foakes-Jackson, *Saint Paul*, pp. 128–48.
2. McNeile, A. H., *St. Paul*, pp. 50–64.
3. Wood, C. T., *Life of Paul*, pp. 98–109.
4. Ramsay, *St. Paul the Traveller*, pp. 213–36.
5. Kent, *Work and Teachings of the Apostles*, pp. 104–5; 112–19.
6. Gilbert, *Student's Life of Paul*, pp. 107–25.
7. Conybeare and Howson, *Life and Epistles of St. Paul*, chaps. viii, ix.
8. Farrar, *Life and Work of St. Paul*, chaps. xxv, xxvi.
9. *Bible for Home and School*, "Acts," pp. 154–67.
10. McGiffert, *A History of Christianity in the Apostolic Age*, pp. 234–56.
11. Bacon, *The Story of St. Paul*, pp. 147–63.

CHAPTER VIII

AT ATHENS AND CORINTH

I. AT ATHENS

In company with his new friends from Beroea Paul voyaged southward past Mount Olympus and along the shores of Greece to the harbor of Athens. There his companions left him. Though his words in I Thess. 3:1 may have been written with reference to a later part of his stay, they apply equally well to the first days after his arrival. He was "at Athens alone."

There was much in this city that might have made it attractive to Paul as a place to tarry a while and to work. It was the home of athletics, art, philosophy, and religion. In the great stadium, which has in modern times been restored to its ancient splendor, were held the famous Greek games. Paul was not a little interested in athletics, and in his letters often made effective use of references to boxing and wrestling, to training for contests, to racing, and to the winning of prizes.

Athens was the most artistically built city in the world. Its profusion of gracefully carved statues and wonderfully ornamented temples and public buildings made it almost a fairy city. The Parthenon, the crown of the Acropolis, was a marvel of architecture. Even in its ruin it has a suggestion of beauty which can scarcely be paralleled.

Athens was famous also as a center of philosophy. Socrates, Plato, and Aristotle had given a great impetus to thinking and reasoning on the meaning of life, the immortality of the soul, and the nature of God. Many philosophical sects had arisen. The Epicureans (Acts 17:18), while not denying the possible existence of gods, held that sense-perception is the only basis of knowledge and that the gods had nothing to do with human affairs. The Stoics (Acts 17:18), on the other hand, believed that every man possesses within him a spark of the divine reason, and so is in a sense akin to God.

Partly because it was such a center of philosophy, Athens was also a gathering-place for many different religions and religious beliefs. The old religion of Zeus was losing its hold upon the Greeks. The twelve gods on Mount Olympus were no longer as real as they once had been. But for that very reason other religions found a place. The multiplicity of altars and worships must have been bewildering to almost any visitor. One of the largest and loftiest temples in the city was built by Antiochus Epiphanes, king of Syria. Antiochus had lived and reigned in Antioch, so named after his family, the same city from which Paul had set out upon this missionary tour. Antioch and Athens were not utterly unknown to each other, as Paul would at once recognize when he visited this temple close by the Acropolis. On the contrary there were many points of contact, and not least was the message which he himself was bringing.

Paul determined to make only a brief stay. The implication of Acts 17:16 is that he was not expecting to undertake any definite program of establishing here a Christian community. He was "waiting" for Silas and Timothy. Perhaps there was not a large enough or popular enough Jewish synagogue to furnish a basis of a large work. Perhaps he had reason to think the Jews here would be especially hostile. More probably, however, he had for some time had his mind set upon Corinth as the best center in which to establish the gospel in Greece. In Macedonia also he had passed through important cities, such as Amphipolis, without preaching. He waited in Athens only because he wished to have Silas and Timothy with him when he went to Corinth that they might all begin there together.

But while he waited his spirit was provoked within him at seeing the city so "full of idols." He determined to use the little time he had in planting the seed of truth here. Following his usual custom he began in the synagogue with the Jews and with that outer circle of "devout persons." He reasoned also wherever he found opportunity with those whom he met in the market-place. Here some of the philosophers, both Epicureans and Stoics, heard bits of his teaching and passed the word to others. Some understood Paul to speak of "Jesus" and the "Resurrection" as two powers or divinities, much as they had been accustomed to hear of Attis and

Adonis, or Isis and Osiris. The word "divinities" of
Acts 17:18 suggests that many conceived the Spirit of
Jesus to be an indwelling voice similar to the "divine
spirit" about which Socrates had talked. Verse 18 uses
the same word which Socrates used.

They requested that Paul give a public presentation
of his teaching before the council of the Areopagus—the
same city which had in that earlier, less tolerant day
condemned Socrates to drink the hemlock for introducing
new "divinities" in the Greek religion. This was Paul's
opportunity. While Luke's account of Paul's speech
would not fill two minutes in speaking, it is suggestive
of many things which Paul may have said. The altar
"to an unknown god" was not an unusual object.
When success had attended a man in a business project
or in time of personal danger, he was sometimes doubtful which of the gods it would be most appropriate to
honor in his expression of gratitude. In 1910, during
excavations at Pergamum in Asia Minor, a stone was
discovered bearing an inscription which should probably
be read: "To the Unknown Gods." Such an inscription furnished Paul an excellent starting-point.

But the altar served only to introduce Paul's strong
appeal to that deeper longing and searching described
in chapter i of this volume. Popular Greek philosophies
and religions had long been endeavoring to "feel after"
and "find" that spiritual Lord who dwelleth not in
temples made with hands. The quotation, "For we
are also his offspring," is from the Greek poet Aratus,
who had lived near Tarsus, Paul's birthplace. While
the name of Christ is not mentioned in the record of the
address, the omission is perhaps of little significance in

view of the forceful and effective closing contrast between the former times of ignorance and the present call to repentance.

Accustomed to the teachings of the religions current in Greek cities, Paul's hearers would understand his message to be an invitation to join a new society in which the power of a divine spirit would enable all participants to rise above the power of death and judgment into a life of mystic communion with God both here and hereafter. Some asked to have him speak again and explain further, but probably "devout" Greeks were not many in Athens. Paul was among people whose moral and religious sense had become accustomed to continually hearing new teachings. Although one member of the Areopagus and some others became converts, Paul decided that further efforts here would not be the best use of his time. He accordingly set out for Corinth without waiting longer for Silas and Timothy.

2. A YEAR AND A HALF AT CORINTH

Corinth had two harbors, one opening toward the east and one toward the west. It was on the main route from Rome and Italy to Asia Minor and Syria. The canal, three and a half miles long, through the rock of the isthmus, begun by Julius Caesar, continued by Nero, and finished in 1893, must have been in Paul's day one of the city improvements much discussed and keenly anticipated. At that time it was by a wooden railway that the endless cargoes of merchandise were transshipped. Such a strategic location for a commercial and industrial center was unparalleled in the Roman world.

In 146 B.C., because of its leadership of an Achaian league against Rome, the city was largely destroyed, and for a hundred years was little more than a ruin. It was rebuilt and in 46 B.C. made a Roman colony by Julius Caesar. Paul found it in a time of great industrial expansion. It was full of people from every nation. Its gold had increased, and with the increase of wealth and commerce had come the increase of vice and materialism.

A considerable part of the temple of Apollo survived the sack of the Romans; part survived also the devastating earthquake of 1858. The seven remaining columns measure nearly 25 feet high and nearly 6 feet in diameter at the base. Paul would know at once by its tapering columns and its peculiar type of architecture that it was an "ancient" temple. It was in fact six hundred years old when Paul arrived. This holy temple, perhaps in ruins, may conceivably have furnished him some such starting-point as was offered in Athens by the altar to the unknown god.

One other outstanding feature of Corinth should be noted. Acro-Corinthus, that great mass of rock upon which the well-nigh impregnable citadel of Corinth was located, rises sharply to a height of 1,800 feet. The far-reaching view east and west would suggest anew to Paul the strategic importance of so planting the gospel here that it should never be uprooted. For from Corinth and its continually changing population the message would be carried by sailors and travelers both westward and eastward to every port of the Mediterranean. It would be worth while to stay longer here than at any other center which he had thus far visited.

For a prolonged stay it was necessary for him to find a home and opportunity to work at his trade. He was fortunate in finding such congenial companions as Aquila, a Jew of Pontus, and his wife Priscilla. Suetonius says that Claudius expelled the Jews from Rome because they were stirred up by a certain agitator among them named "Chrestus." This was possibly a popular perversion of the name Christ. Expelled from Rome, Aquila and Priscilla had taken up their stay in the nearest large city outside of Italy. During Paul's stay with them in Corinth they would be of great help, especially during the absence of Silas and Timothy. Possibly they brought the news that there were Christians in Rome, and by their descriptions of that imperial city increased Paul's determination to go there when the opportunity proved suitable.

The superscription over the door of the synagogue in which Paul preached has probably been preserved. In the Museum at Corinth is today the stone with the writing, "Synagogue of the Hebrews." The plain character of the block and the rough unprofessional style of the lettering, suggesting that the Jews were not among the aristocrats of the city, are an instructive commentary on Paul's words in I Cor. 1:26, "Not many wise after the flesh, not many mighty, not many noble."

The arrival of Silas and Timothy from Macedonia brought cheer to Paul's soul (I Thess. 3:6, 7). Paul had not only missed their companionship and assistance, but had been anxious for news of the Macedonian churches. Whether Timothy came to Athens from Beroea and was then sent back to Thessalonica, as

I Thess. 3:1, 2 suggests, or was left behind at Beroea with instructions to go to Thessalonica, and thence to join Paul at Corinth, as Acts suggests, need not be decided. In any case, Silas and Timothy arrived at Corinth and Paul's spirit was refreshed. Quite possibly while Timothy had been at Thessalonica Silas had been at Philippi, and now perhaps brought with him the much-appreciated gift from the Philippians to Paul mentioned in II Cor. 11:9 and Phil. 4:15.

After the arrival of Silas and Timothy, Paul's preaching took on increased vigor. The narrower Jews were alarmed and "opposed themselves." Leaving the synagogue Paul and his companions found warm welcome again among that outer circle of "the fearers of God." Titus Justus, who offered his house as a meeting-place, conveniently located next door to the synagogue, is designated as one of this outer circle by the phrase in Acts 18:7, "one that worshiped God." Even the ruler of the synagogue, Crispus, who not unnaturally would be a broad-minded man, also joined the new society. Paul mentions him in I Cor. 1:14 as one of the very few whom he personally baptized.

For a year and six months Paul's work among the people of Corinth prospered. With its population of about two hundred thousand freemen and perhaps as many slaves, Corinth was full of all the evils of a big city. In fact the moral level was exceptionally low even for that day. "To live like a Corinthian" was, from the time of Aristophanes, a phrase used both in Greek and Latin to express immorality. The Greek democratic spirit went to excess in the midst of the ever-changing population. From the west came the gladiatorial shows and the evils of Roman society; from the east came the impure oriental worship of Astarte, perverting the Greek worship of Aphrodite. Drunkenness and reveling were common. It was at Corinth that Paul wrote the description in Rom., chap. 1, of the condition of men who know not God. "Professing themselves to be wise, they became fools . . . . being filled with all unrighteousness, wickedness, covetousness . . . . full of envy, murder, strife, deceit . . . . inventors of evil things . . . . covenant breakers . . . ."

The contrast between the actual life of the Corinthians and the new nobility of ideal which Paul presented was heaven high. Under his leadership some of them in the midst of their days of shiploading or other toil met from time to time to exhort each other to higher living. Paul told them that their bodies were temples wherein the spirit of God dwells. This spirit was conceived by many in a crass way, and many felt that to be carried away by an ecstasy and to utter strange sounds after the manner of the Greek oracles was a supreme manifestation of the spirit. Yet under the untiring leadership of Paul the circle of Christians must have learned much and lived much of the Christian teaching. He was continually pleading with them to die with Christ to the flesh and rise with him into a new life of spiritual communion with God. The great poem on brotherly love in I Cor., chap. 13, is a suggestion of the exalted goal which he held ever before them. "Love suffereth long and is kind . . . . doth not behave itself unseemly, seeketh not its own . . . . taketh not account of evil, rejoiceth not in unrighteousness . . . . beareth all things . . . . hopeth all things."

Paul had probably not intended at first to remain a long time in Corinth (cf. I Thess. 3:11; 2:18), but the difficulty and responsibility of his task held him. He did not abate his efforts, for the Lord whom he had seen on the road to Damascus he saw again "in the night by a vision" and heard him saying, "Be not afraid, for I am with thee." At the end of a year and six months, evidently at the time of the arrival of a new proconsul, the Jews thought it an opportune time for a determined effort to stop this propaganda which was becoming such a formidable rival of the synagogue.

But the new proconsul was brother of the great Stoic philosopher Seneca. The situation was very different from that which Paul had encountered in Lystra. He had traveled beyond the zone of the tyranny of the Jews. In Corinth Paul won a clear victory. Gallio refused to listen to the complaints against him. When they persisted he drove them from the court. Then he showed his utter disdain for such religious jealousy by allowing the crowd to seize Sosthenes the arch-persecutor and give him such a beating as in earlier days Paul had suffered at Philippi. This Sosthenes, ruler of the synagogue, was probably just such a narrow-minded man as would be chosen to take the place of the converted Crispus, the ruler of the synagogue, whom Paul had personally baptized (I Cor. 1:14).

The dating of the proconsulship of Gallio is one of the most interesting chapters of modern archaeology. Thus far in the journeys of Paul there has been no statement that would enable us to date an event of Paul's life in terms of Roman history. Even in regard to the proconsulship of Gallio, Wendt made the statement as late as 1899 in the revised *Meyer Commentary* that we have no evidence outside the Book of Acts that Gallio was proconsul. In 1908 Deissmann in his *Light from the Ancient East* wrote that as yet no inscription had been found for dating Gallio's term of office. But in April, 1908, in the *Report of the Palestine Exploration Fund* appeared a description of four broken pieces of stone found at Delphi in Greece. These four pieces, one of which was published as early as 1895, when brought together, have been found to be parts of an imperial letter of the time of Claudius. On one piece appears a part of the name and titles of Claudius. On a second fragment occurs the date within the reign of Claudius, his twenty-sixth acclamation as emperor. A third fragment contains the name of Gallio. The fourth fragment contains a part of the title proconsul.

From the assembled inscription read in the light of related facts of Roman history it appears that Gallio was proconsul from the summer of 51 to the summer of 52. Reckoning back a year and six months from the accession of Gallio we reach the beginning of the year 50 as the date of Paul's arrival in Corinth. Incidentally this accords with the statement of Orosius vii. 6, 15, quoting Josephus, that Claudius expelled the Jews from Rome in his ninth year, that is in the year 49. Aquila and Priscilla had come only "lately" from Rome, as Luke writes in Acts 18:2. (For further discussion of the inscription and date see Deissmann, *St. Paul*, Appendix II; also *American Journal of Theology*, XXI [1917], 299, last paragraph.)

3. TWO LETTERS TO THE THESSALONIANS

When Timothy came to Corinth from Thessalonica (cf. p. 135) he brought news from the circle of disciples Paul had so abruptly left in Thessalonica, which in one respect was unexpected. Paul had told the Thessalonians that their new life in Christ and their possession of the Spirit made them victors over death. He had assured them of eternal life and of a future Kingdom of love and brotherhood soon to be established upon the earth. They had not unnaturally understood Paul to say that they would all live to share in that future Kingdom. They were now in great distress over the fact that some of their number had died and apparently would not share the joy of the coming commonwealth. They were perhaps asking dubiously whether the coming of Jesus might not be so long postponed that none of them would share in its glory.

Not wishing to interrupt his strenuous activity in Corinth, Paul sat down and wrote them a letter. Or, to be more accurate, he paced the floor in his intensity of feeling as he dictated a letter. For Paul was a nervous man and usually had his letters written in the ordinary way by a professional writer. This was perhaps Paul's first letter of length to a Greek church, and he shows by his superlative language how deeply the success of the gospel in a Greek city had impressed him. It was no mere formal custom which made him express his thankfulness at the beginning of every letter except Galatians. He probably experienced a genuine sense of surprise and gratification at the welcome which was accorded to his gospel.

After his salutation and expression of gratitude (1:1–10) he goes on to tell them how completely and personally he devoted himself to their welfare (2:1–12) and again refers gratefully to their response (2:13–16). He assures them of his longing to visit them (2:17–20) and of the joy which Timothy's news afforded him (3:1–10). He ends this part of his letter with a benediction (3:11–13). In the second half of the letter he gives them exhortations to nobler and cleaner living (4:1–12), and especially to faith in the resurrection of those who have fallen asleep (4:13–18) and to watchfulness and readiness for the coming of the Lord (5:1–11). After further general Christian admonition (5:12–22) he closes with a benediction and a request that the letter be read to all the brethren (5:23–28).

Although he told them in his polite way, "Ye have no need that one write unto you" (4:9), his letter must have been very welcome to the church. His words of comfort concerning those who were "fallen asleep" are in striking contrast to that papyrus letter quoted in chapter i of this volume: "I wept over the death of your son as much as I did when my own child passed away . . . . against such things one can do nothing." While such dispiriting letters were being written from friend to friend in Thessalonica, Paul was picturing the glorious hope of the resurrection and pleading with his friends, "Sorrow not even as the rest who have no hope."

The second letter was written two or three months after the first. Both were probably written within the year 50. The effect of the first letter had been more than Paul anticipated. The situation had almost reversed itself. Some at least of the Thessalonians had gone to the other extreme. They had decided that, as the King-dom was immediately impending, therefore there was no need to "work at all" or earn a living. They could get something to eat at the Christian suppers, and in general live from the generosity of their brothers (II Thess. 3:11).

In this second letter he expresses thanks for their growth in faith and love in the midst of persecution (1:1–12). Then he turns at once to the chief occasion of his writing. They should not think that "the day of the Lord is now present," for some time must first elapse (2:1–12). After exhorting them to stand fast (2:13–17) and uttering a few words of prayer for them (3:1–5) he tells them not to be carried away into disorderly con-duct, but to keep quietly on with their work (3:6–15). In concluding he calls attention to his personal greeting and benediction in his own handwriting (3:16–18).

The genuineness of this second letter has sometimes been called in question. In the first letter there is an emphasis upon the nearness of the Second Coming (4:15–17; 5:2), while in the second the emphasis is upon the fact that a time must intervene before the coming (2:2, 3). It is conceivable that someone after Paul's death, feeling that Paul was mistaken concerning the nearness of the coming, wished to save Paul's reputa-tion or to correct a popular opinion. But it is just as likely that Paul would wish to correct a false opinion or a wrong attitude as that some later writer would do so. This and other arguments advanced are not sufficient to prove that Paul did not write the letter.

Each of these letters on reaching Thessalonica was "read unto all the brethren," as Paul requested in

I Thess. 5:26. After the reading it was handed over to the treasurer or other officer of the church who for safe keeping put it away with his accounts and receipts, until one day, after Paul's death, someone going around to the churches to collect the writings of Paul found the letters and made a copy of them.

4. BRIEF VISIT TO EPHESUS

If, as stated above, the Jewish demonstration at Corinth took place soon after Gallio became proconsul in the summer of 51 A.D., it was probably in the early fall of 51 that Paul left Corinth to return to the East. The little visit to Ephesus is of significance in the light of his subsequent return to the city for a stay of three years. As he stopped on his way eastward he found a warm welcome and received a request to stay longer.

Picturing to himself the possibilities of the gospel in this greatest of the cities which he had yet entered, he hastened on his homeward journey. The two friends, Aquila and Priscilla, with whom he had lived so long in Corinth and who had accompanied him to Ephesus he was now able to leave in charge when he departed. Luke devotes only two verses of his narrative to Paul's journey eastward and back again. Landing at Caesarea, the Roman port of Jerusalem, Paul went up to salute the mother-church. Perhaps he found time for a visit at his sister's home and for a brief recital of his adventures to his Jerusalem friends.

Arrived again at Antioch he had completed on this second missionary journey considerably more than two thousand miles. Having left Antioch in the spring of 49, and reaching Antioch again in the winter at the end of 51 or the beginning of 52, he had spent nearly three years on the journey. Three important and strategic Christian centers he had founded, at Philippi, at Thessalonica, and at Corinth.

5. THE LETTER TO THE GALATIANS

As explained above in chapter vii the recipients of the letter "to the Galatians" were probably the converts of the churches founded on the first missionary journey in the southern part of the Roman province of Galatia. These churches of Derbe, Lystra, Iconium, and Pisidian Antioch he visited a second time on his second journey. In the letter he speaks of his preaching on the "former" occasion (4:13) in such way as to indicate that he had visited them twice. If the two visits were the going and returning on the first journey the letter was written in the year 49 at Antioch. If the second visit was that of the second journey it was written perhaps at Antioch in 52.

The occasion of the letter was a crisis which had arisen in the churches over the question of circumcision. It was perhaps the greatest crisis which Paul ever faced among his churches. The Judaizers, defeated at Jerusalem, were at work in Galatia. With deadly effectiveness they were using all those arguments noted in chapter vi in connection with the Jerusalem conference.

The Galatian converts had been living the gospel of freedom as Paul had preached it to them. "Ye were running well," he tells them (5:7). But it was apparently easy to lose faith in an absent leader. The Judaizers made the most of the situation. They saw what a success the new faith was. They were determined to annex it to the synagogue for the glorification of Judaism. Moreover, they regarded a gospel of liberty and freedom as not merely un-Jewish but as a positive encouragement to a lower moral standard.

Paul heard that his new converts, alarmed by the arguments of the Judaizers, were already "removing" from the gospel which he had preached. He realized the critical character of the situation. In his indignation that the Judaizers should thus even after the Jerusalem conference be undermining his work, he wrote a letter which for personal sharpness of statement and vigorous effectiveness is hardly excelled either among Paul's letters or the letters of any other man. Although some of its statements were so peculiarly adapted to the readers of Galatia that we in America do not catch their force, no one can study the epistle without feeling the power of the personality behind it. It is first-hand testimony to a great conflict, a voice out of the midst of battle.

The first two chapters are a rare bit of autobiography. Paul had no desire to write about himself. But the Judaizers had attacked his apostleship. They reasoned with the Galatians that the twelve apostles were the ones who had been with Jesus and who knew his gospel. Anything which Paul preached he must have received from them. And where he differed from them he had no real authority for his preaching. Paul's answer was to narrate the salient facts of his career so far as they concerned the source of his gospel. The circumstances preceding and surrounding his conversion (Gal., chap. 1), his independent position at the Jerusalem conference (2:1–10), his subsequent rebuke of Peter (2:11–21), all showed that his gospel was from Christ independently received and not from men. The apostles themselves had recognized this in giving him the right hand of fellowship.

In chapters 3 and 4 he turns from the personal side to arguments respecting his gospel itself. The Judaizers had evidently been arguing from Gen. 17:7 and other passages that God's promises of future blessings were explicitly limited to Abraham and his descendants. Paul's answer is "Abraham believed God." That was his righteousness, as the Jewish Scriptures plainly state. Those who maintain an attitude of faith toward God such as Abraham had are the true "sons of Abraham," not those who accept circumcision. The Book of Genesis itself has the distinct statement: "In thee shall all the nations be blessed." The promises were explicitly meant for all the world (3:1–9). Moreover, on the basis of law every man is cursed who is not legally perfect; hence the Scripture itself says "the righteous shall live by faith" (3:10–14). The covenant with Abraham was not on the basis of law, because the law was not in existence till four hundred and thirty years after Abraham (3:15–22), nor was the covenant displaced by law.

The Judaizers must have felt the sting of Paul's irony if they read or heard his next statement that the law was only for schoolboys, a sort of "guardian" or "tutor" to lead along those who are undeveloped. Circumcision was after all not really a very adult way of exhibiting one's religion. Now that faith has come "we are no longer under a tutor." We have become of age, no longer "children," but "sons" of God (3:23—4:11). He appeals to the Galatians in the name of their former loyalty not to fall victims to these crafty teachers. Thinking, perhaps, of that incident in Lystra when he was hailed as Mercury, the messenger of the gods, he reminds them in touching words that they received him as "an angel of God" (4:12–20). He closes this part of his letter with a last argument based on an allegorical interpretation of the story of Sarah and Hagar (4:21–31).

In the last two chapters he exhorts them to stand fast in their freedom (5:1–12), to avoid turning liberty into license, to seek the fruits of the spirit, love, joy, faithfulness, temperance (5:13–26), to be not weary in well-doing (6:1–10). He adds a whole paragraph in his own big handwriting (6:11–18) warning against the Judaizers and closing with a reference to the marks of Jesus upon his body, meaning perhaps the scars received at his stoning in Lystra.

Galatians is the Christian charter of freedom. It marks a new epoch in the history of religion. Paul took a new and courageous stand in saying to these very human and fallible Christians of Lystra and of other cities that liberty is one of the greatest words in religion, that obedience to written law is quite a lower stage, that he who lives in Christ is above formal codes of command and prohibition. He was speaking out of his own deep experience and conviction. It was a somewhat similar, though quite distinct, truth which Luther had in mind when he said in his tract on Christian liberty: "Good works do not make a good man, but a good man does good works." First the spirit was Paul's great teaching, then the fruits of the spirit.

SUPPLEMENTARY READING

1. Foakes-Jackson, *Saint Paul*, pp. 149–58.
2. McNeile, A. H., *St. Paul*, pp. 64–76; 121–35; 168–81.
3. Wood, C. T., *Life of Paul*, pp. 64–91; 109–45.

4. Ramsay, *St. Paul the Traveller*, pp. 237–61.
5. Kent, *Work and Teachings of the Apostles*, pp. 125–32; 135–42; 106–9.
6. Gilbert, *Student's Life of Paul*, pp. 125–41.
7. Conybeare and Howson, *Life and Epistles of St. Paul*, chaps. x–xiii.
8. Farrar, *Life and Work of St. Paul*, chaps. xxvii, xxviii.
9. *Bible for Home and School*, "Acts," pp. 167–76.
10. Jones, *St. Paul the Orator*, pp. 80–106.
11. McGiffert, *A History of Christianity in the Apostolic Age*, pp. 256–73; also pp. 217–30.
12. Bacon, *Story of St. Paul*, pp. 163–73; 236–65.

ON THESSALONIAN LETTERS AND GALATIANS

13. Burton, *Handbook of the Life of the Apostle Paul*, pp. 45–57.
14. Goodspeed, *Story of the New Testament*, pp. 1–13.
15. Moffatt, *Introduction to the New Testament*, pp. 64–107.

CHAPTER IX

AT EPHESUS

1. Arrival at Ephesus
   Acts 18:23; 19:1
2. Disciples of John the Baptist
   Acts 18:24—19:7
3. Three Years of Activity
   Acts 19:8-20, 26; 20:18-35; I Cor. 4:11-13
4. Departure from Ephesus
   Acts 19:21—20:1; I Cor. 15:32; II Cor. 1:8, 9

1. ARRIVAL AT EPHESUS

Probably not long after sending off the letter to the Galatians Paul departed from Antioch on a third missionary journey. Undoubtedly he stopped for a night at his home in Tarsus. Then he hastened on through the Galatian country, including also the Phrygian cities of Iconium and Antioch (18:23).[1] This time he was not forbidden by the Holy Spirit to speak the word in Asia, but went directly to the heart of the life of that province.

The city of Ephesus was the largest, richest, and most influential city in which Paul founded a church. His success here was the climax of his labors. The province of Asia, of which Ephesus was the capital, was one of the wealthiest of the Roman Empire. Six centuries before Paul's time Croesus had accumulated his vast treasures at Sardis. Smyrna and Miletus were important centers of culture and commerce.

[1] τὴν Γαλατικὴν χώραν καὶ Φρυγίαν.

Ephesus owed its special pre-eminence in no small measure to its natural advantages of location. The Maeander River in its "meandering" course toward the sea makes a sharp turn a few miles before reaching the shore and flows southward for many miles parallel to the coast. The result was that the rich commerce from the interior and from the east following down the valley of the Maeander found it easier to cross a small ridge to Ephesus on the coast than to turn south along the river to its mouth at Miletus. The modern railroad in like manner built along the Maeander has its station at Ephesus. Since Ephesus was located also on a good-sized river of its own, the Caÿster, it thus had a double advantage.

The city was, like Athens, artistically laid out, with finely paved streets and large public buildings. The theater, one of the largest in Asia Minor and today one of the best preserved, was centrally located. The seats were arranged in rows upon the side of a small hill partly hollowed out. This theater faced west and commanded a good view of the harbor a mile away. In a straight line from the theater to the harbor ran the main street, beautifully colonnaded on both sides. Along this street were the lecture halls, libraries, and minor temples, so massively built that their ruins still line both sides of the old pavement. On this street was located in all probability the school of Tyrannus, which Paul secured for his use.

In front of the theater was another principal thoroughfare running north and south. It was at the junction of the two streets at the market-place in front of the theater that the multitude gathered for the demonstration against Paul. On this latter street somewhat to the north was the Greek stadium, measuring an eighth of a mile from end to end, holding six thousand people. Here or in the theater prisoners fought with wild beasts in the arena, as Paul, perhaps metaphorically, says he was compelled to fight at Ephesus (I Cor. 15:32).

The Temple of Diana was located at a distance from the business center of the city. The place had been sacred from very early times. Its oracle was almost as famous as that of Delphi in Greece. The temple built upon this ancient and holy spot was so marvelous in its splendor and elaborateness that it was numbered as one of the seven wonders of the world. The edifice was in Paul's day at least five centuries old. It had been built by the Greeks and dedicated to the worship of the goddess Artemis, afterward identified with the Roman Diana. The floor of the temple, which was approached by steps on each side, measured about 350 feet in length by 150 feet in breadth. The columns of the temple towered 60 feet above this platform and were visible far out to sea.

Many legends had gathered around this ancient center of Greek worship. The early priestesses of the temple were perhaps connected with the rise of some of the stories of the Amazon women in Greek mythology. The image of the goddess of the temple was in Paul's day said to have fallen directly out of heaven (Acts 19:35). According to this legend the image was the only perfect likeness of the goddess. Hence it was that the thousands of pilgrims who came to worship, or to consult the oracle, took home with them a copy of the sacred statue. The poorest pilgrims bought copies of terra cotta, the more prosperous ones copies of marble, while the wealthy tourists could afford silver ones. Demetrius catered to the wealthy class.

Because the temple was held so sacred it had many uses besides that of worship. Those who had money or valuables considered it the safest place in Ephesus, and deposited their treasures there. The temple had become in Paul's day the safety-deposit vault of Ephesus. Moreover, since its precincts were held inviolable, many fugitives of the empire, both of the nobility and of the people, found here a place of refuge. Its fame in this respect spread far and wide. No doubt the slave Onesimus, who ran away from his master Philemon in Colossae and was afterward converted and sent back by Paul, found refuge for a while here. The life of Ephesus was affected so widely through the various channels of temple activity—pilgrims, tourists, refugees, priests, singers, servants, guides, image-makers, bankers—that Ephesus was called the "keeper" of the temple of the heaven-sent image (Acts 19:35).

2. DISCIPLES OF JOHN THE BAPTIST

When Paul arrived at Ephesus his first activity, Luke tells us, was among the followers of John the Baptist. This sect, which Paul may have encountered often before in his travels, was perhaps particularly strong here. Its members proclaimed John as founder of their faith. They seem to have given a prominent place to Jesus and some of his teachings. Perhaps they spoke of him as John's chief disciple and interpreter. But they regarded the Baptist as the greater, and around his preaching they built up their religion.

Our reports of John's preaching indicate that he announced a speedily coming judgment which was to fall upon the Jews. While his principal warning was to Jews, he may by inference have included the other nations also in his picture of the judgment. In view of this coming judgment John urged repentance, for repentance would save from the punishment which would come upon the unrepentant. After repentance he enjoined purity of moral life.

This may well have been the message of his followers, and so far as our information goes they may have addressed this message chiefly or even exclusively to Jews. It is natural to suppose that the acceptance of this message of coming judgment would not be accompanied by those enthusiastic and ecstatic experiences which among Christian believers were known as the gifts of the Spirit. Since these followers of John did not accept the messiahship of Jesus, they did not of course look for the return of Jesus from heaven as the Christ. The repeated insistence in the Gospel of John that the Baptist was not the Christ is perhaps an evidence that John was regarded as the Christ by his followers. But there is no reason to think that they were apocalyptists or looked for the coming of John from heaven. They had no expectation of a second coming either of Jesus or of John. Apparently the movement was a prophetic and ethical one, quite without the enthusiasm and without the vivid apocalyptic hope of the Christian movement.

This John-the-Baptist propaganda was one of the closest rivals of early Christianity. Each recognized the prophet of the other, but each claimed primacy for its own leader. The Gospel of John, written long after

Paul's death, never refers to the Baptist without emphasizing that he was not the Christ, that he was only a prophet, inferior to Jesus, but bearing witness to the superiority of Jesus. The evidence of the Acts account, the fuller evidence of the Gospel of John, and the later evidence of other literature combine to indicate that Johannism existed side by side with Christianity from the very beginning and for several centuries at least.

Apollos was one of the chief missionaries of the sect at Ephesus. He was a well-educated man from the great center of learning, Alexandria. He was an eloquent speaker and able to use the Jewish Scriptures in argument with powerful effect. Priscilla and Aquila—her name often precedes that of her husband, as though she were somewhat of a leader—had in Paul's absence become acquainted with Apollos and converted him to the Christian point of view.

As though to complete the work of his two friends, Paul upon his arrival in Ephesus went among the disciples of John to win as many of them as possible. Probably in a conciliatory way he told them that a baptism of repentance was negatively good, but that they lacked the positive side of baptism into the name of Jesus and of possession by the Spirit. He brought over twelve men to the Christian circle of believers. But the sect remained, as stated above, a strong and active body.

Thus Paul had to work in Ephesus as elsewhere in competition with many rivals. The old mythology and idolatry were strongly intrenched. The Temple of Diana was one of the seven wonders of the world. To those whose belief in mythology had waned Judaism offered a more spiritual and truly ethical worship. If Judaism lacked a certain mystical element which the philosophically minded craved, there were the mystery-religions, promising not only present communion with deity but future immortality. In especially close competition with Paul's work were the two reformed Jewish sects, legalistic Christianity, which was a slightly Christianized Pharisaism, and the sect described above which followed the preaching of John.

3. THREE YEARS OF ACTIVITY

Ephesus was Paul's greatest opportunity and Paul's greatest achievement. An incidental reference in Acts 20:31 states that the length of his stay was "three years," but this may mean simply that he was there more than two years. This was his longest stop of which we have any record. After his first work among the disciples of John the Baptist he devoted three months to the Jewish synagogue, then for two years he reasoned daily in the school of Tyrannus.

He made Ephesus a center for spreading the gospel throughout all the province of Asia, as stated in Acts 19:10. He has immortalized the name of his first convert in Asia by mentioning him in Rom. 16:5, "Epaenetus my beloved, who is the firstfruits of Asia unto Christ." This man was probably a resident of Ephesus. But Paul thought of Ephesus only as the center of a great province. Up the valley of the Maeander the gospel went as far as Colossae. There Philemon became a Christian and later received a personal letter from Paul.

Epaphras, a fellow-worker who went forth and founded the church at Colossae, is mentioned by Paul in Col. 1:6, 7. Perhaps all of the seven churches of Asia Minor to whom the seven letters of the Book of Revelation were addressed were founded at this time by Paul and his supporters. As the sailors and merchants at Corinth carried the gospel to distant places, so probably in Ephesus the innumerable pilgrims to the Temple of Diana carried the seed of the gospel back to their homes in the cities of Asia and also to neighboring provinces.

The school of Tyrannus, to which Paul went after his three months at the synagogue, was probably a lecture hall used during the morning hours for philosophical and scientific instruction. In that hot climate it was customary to begin work early so as to have the burden of the day's work done by eleven o'clock. Thus it would be easy for Paul to hold his discourses during the comparative leisure of the afternoon. This program also gave Paul an opportunity to work at his trade with Aquila and Priscilla during the morning hours. Possibly Tyrannus, the head of the school or college, was inclined to approve Paul's gospel and generously assisted by offering the use of his hall.

A great part of Paul's work was also done toward sunset and in the evening, when he personally visited one home and another. In his address to the Ephesian elders he lays chief emphasis upon this latter side of his activity. "Serving the Lord with all lowliness of mind . . . . I shrank not from declaring unto you anything that was profitable. . . . . From house to house testifying both to Jews and Greeks . . . . I ceased not to admonish everyone night and day with tears. . . . . These hands ministered unto my necessity. I gave you an example that ye ought to help the weak" (Acts 20:18-35).

Paul became known as the friend of the people, the one who comforted the afflicted and bereaved, telling of the sufferings of Christ and of the glory of the resurrection. Doubtless he often gave of his own hard-earned money to relieve poverty and misery as well as dispensed strength and courage to any who were sick or diseased or mentally distressed. Afflicted ones whom Paul could not find time to visit were helped and even sometimes cured by a scarf or handkerchief or any token which represented to them the beneficent power of this man whom they so idealized and perhaps idolized.

The story of the seven sons of Sceva shows that these wandering Jewish exorcists had strayed from home religiously as well as geographically. They probably made considerable money at their evil art of casting spells about people, reciting formulas which called upon evil spirits to come forth, and claiming generally to perform magic cures through the naming of unseen powers who heal and bless. Recent finds of papyri have yielded many examples of these formulas. Among them are some of these peculiarly Jewish forms. Among the Jewish forms the following is one which would seem to fit the description of Acts 19:13. It undertakes by a magic use of the name of Jesus to frighten away evil spirits.

A notable spell for driving out demons. Invocation to be uttered over the head (of the possessed one). Place before him branches of olive, and standing behind him say: Hail, spirit of Abraham; hail, spirit of Isaac; hail, spirit of Jacob; Jesus the Christ, the holy one, the spirit . . . . drive forth the devil from this man, until this unclean demon of Satan shall flee before thee. I adjure thee, O demon, whoever thou art, by the God Sabar-barbathioth Sabarbarbathiuth Sabarbarbathioneth Sabarbar-baphai. Come forth, O demon, whoever thou art, and depart from so-and-so at once, at once, now. Come forth, O demon, for I chain thee with adamantine chains not to be loosed, and I give you over to black chaos in utter destruction [Milligan, *Greek Papyri*, No. 47].

The wandering Jews, or at least two of them, when they tried their new up-to-date formula containing the name of the latest divinity, met with an unexpected reception. The one upon whom they tried it had prob-ably heard of Paul and had gained some idea of his spirit and sympathy. The contrast between Paul's unselfish helpfulness and the money-making schemes of these men, and the even greater contrast between Paul's possible description of the Great Physician and the mo-notonous magic incantations of these exorcists, angered the afflicted man. News of the way in which he attacked the exorcists and put them both to flight spread to the company of Christians and then into the synagogue and to the Greeks of the city.

The burning of the books was the outcome. Luke indicates in Acts 19:18 that some of the Christians them-selves had continued to use magic formulas. Many others were converted by the incident of the exorcist and brought their books. Still others who may have had no special Christian conversion lost faith in the power of incantations generally. Fifty thousand drachmas, about ten thousand dollars, would buy several thousand such books or rolls. When they were all publicly burned the celebration must have been not a small one. It was indeed a far greater blow at magic than the conversion of the ventriloquist girl at Philippi. As at Philippi, so here at Ephesus, Paul's greatest persecution was to be at the hands of those who made fortunes by exploiting the religious instincts of the people.

Luke was probably not with Paul in Ephesus, for his quotations from his diary do not begin again until the next chapter. He has told us much of Paul's successes and little of his difficulties. We must go to Paul's own letters to find references to what he endured in the great struggle. While at Ephesus he wrote to the Corinthians in I Cor. 16:9: "A great door and effectual is opened unto me, and there are many adversaries." In the same letter in 15:32 are his words that he had "fought with beasts at Ephesus." Shortly after leaving Ephesus he wrote in Rom. 16:4 that Aquila and Priscilla had risked their own lives for his sake. Three verses later he wrote of Andronicus and Junias, his "fellow-prisoners."

The "prison of St. Paul" is one of the prominent ruins existing today at Ephesus. Did Paul actually spend a time in prison here? There is an early Christian tradition that he did. Moreover, in the same year in which he left Ephesus he wrote in II Cor. 1:8 of "our affliction which befell us in Asia . . . . that we despaired even of life. . . . . We had the sentence of death within ourselves . . . . God delivered us out of so great a death." In the same letter in 11:23 he says that he had been very often in prison. The only imprisonment which Luke records up to this time was the brief one at Philippi. Very likely at least one of the many imprisonments occurred at Ephesus.

As Acts gives information of Paul's successes and the epistles afford an insight into some of his hardships, so another later source throws very interesting light upon the spirit and customs of the early Christian converts themselves. The governor of Bithynia, a province adjoining Asia, wrote a letter in the year 110 to the Roman emperor asking how severely he ought to persecute the Christians. The governor was Pliny the Younger, and the letter is No. 96 of his collected epistles. After stating the general situation he continues as follows:

> With those who have been brought before me as Christians I have pursued the following course. I have asked them if they were Christians, and if they have confessed, I have asked them a second and a third time, threatening them with punishment: if they have persisted, I have commanded them to be led away to punishment. For I did not doubt that whatever that might be which they confessed, at any rate pertinacious and inflexible obstinacy ought to be punished. There have been others . . . . who as Roman citizens I have decided should be sent to Rome. . . . . Others accused by an informer . . . . affirmed that this was the sum of their guilt or error: that they had been accustomed to come together on a fixed day before daylight and to sing responsively a song unto Christ as God: and to bind themselves with an oath, not with a view to the commission of some crime, but, on the contrary, that they would not commit theft, nor robbery, nor adultery, that they would not break faith, nor refuse to restore a deposit when asked for it. When they had done these things, their custom was to separate and to assemble again to partake of a meal, common yet harmless (which is not the characteristic of a nefarious superstition).

The "inflexible" loyalty to Christ, the meetings before daylight, the responsive singing, the pledges which they repeated to each other that they would abstain from dishonesty and impurity, their determination never to break a promise, their common meal together symbolizing their mutual brotherliness, all point to the new conception of religion which Paul had brought to these regions. And the same spirit which caused the burning of the books is also reflected in a different and more developed form in the letter of Pliny when he speaks a little later of "the temples which were almost deserted . . . . and the sacred rites which were for a long time interrupted . . . . and fodder for the victims for which hardly a purchaser was to be found."

Ephesus became the greatest center of Christianity between Antioch and Rome. To its circle of seven churches the epistles of Revelation were later addressed. Here the Gospel of John was written for the especial use of the Pauline Christians. Paul's point of view and many of his favorite expressions and teachings are reflected in various ways in that Gospel.

4. DEPARTURE FROM EPHESUS

The public opposition which finally made it advisable for Paul to leave Ephesus was aroused, not by the Jews nor by the priests of the temple, but by those whose business was injured by his presence. Demetrius made and sold the more expensive kind of images or shrines. He aroused the brotherhood of image-makers. It has been well said that the whole affair was the work of an unworthy unit of organized labor. The Roman Empire was more modern in many ways than is usually realized. Inscriptions and papyri tell not only of the labor unions, but also of trusts or corporations and even of the imperial regulation of prices by public proclamation. In Ephesus inscriptions mention in particular the brotherhoods of the workers-in-wool and of the surveyors.

The mob which the silversmiths succeeded in arousing grew beyond their control, so that "the more part knew not wherefore they were come together." When they seized two of Paul's fellow-workers he decided to go to the rescue. With his persuasive words he might have quieted the people. But the Christian company of disciples held him back. They felt he would never return alive.

It is evident that the mob thought that the chief enemies of Artemis and the temple were the Jews. The crowd did not distinguish between Christian Jews, like Paul, and other Jews. It was an anti-Jewish demonstration. Fortunately Alexander was not allowed to make his defense, for he would probably have tried to exonerate the Jews by throwing the blame as far as possible on Paul and his Christians. For two hours the people kept on crying, "Great is Diana of the Ephesians."

The town clerk, or mayor, succeeded in quieting the mob by an appeal to their civic pride, and by a reference to the sharpness of the Roman government in dealing with riots which take the business of the courts into their own hands. Nevertheless, it was advisable for Paul to leave the city. He had been intending for some time to do so, but now he hastened his departure. To remain would only mean further persecution of the Christian community.

As Paul left the city his soul was "weighed down exceedingly." Outwardly at least it looked in some ways as if Diana of the Ephesians had conquered. Almost at the same time he received word that the church at Corinth was on the point of repudiating him. How truly he could write, as he did soon afterward, "the sufferings of Christ abound unto us" (II Cor. 1:5). Would all his labors be undone? We cannot help wishing for his sake that the veil of the following centuries might have been rolled back for a moment that he might have seen the result of his efforts and the fruit of his planting in the final triumph of Christ in the Roman Empire.

SUPPLEMENTARY READING

1. Foakes-Jackson, *Saint Paul*, pp. 159–79.
2. McNeile, A. H., *St. Paul*, pp. 76–86.
3. Wood, C. T., *Life of Paul*, pp. 146–59.
4. Ramsay, *St. Paul the Traveller*, pp. 262–82.
5. Kent, *Work and Teachings of the Apostles*, pp. 173–79.
6. Gilbert, *Student's Life of Paul*, pp. 142–56.
7. Conybeare and Howson, *Life and Epistles of St. Paul*, chaps. xiv–xvi.
8. Farrar, *Life and Work of St. Paul*, chap. xxxi.
9. *Bible for Home and School*, "Acts," pp. 176–87.
10. McGiffert, *A History of Christianity in the Apostolic Age*, pp. 273–90.
11. Bacon, *The Story of St. Paul*, pp. 174–81.

CHAPTER X

FROM EPHESUS TO CORINTH

1. Paul's Correspondence with Corinth
   I Cor. entire; II Cor. entire. For evidence concerning
   the various communications see I Cor. 5:9; 7:1; II Cor.
   2:4, 9; 7:8, 12. The student is also advised to read
   with care I Cor. 1:1—2:5; chaps. 13, 15, 16; II Cor.,
   chapters 10, 13, 9, 2, 7:2–16 (reading in this order)

2. Through Macedonia to Corinth
   Acts 20:1–3; II Cor. 1:15, 16; 2:12, 13; 7:5–7, 11, 16

3. The Epistle to the Romans
   Romans entire. Read with especial care Rom. 15:22–
   33; 3:21–30; 7:7—8:2; 8:18–25, 31–39; chap. 16

4. From Corinth to Jerusalem
   Acts 20:3—21:16

I. PAUL'S CORRESPONDENCE WITH CORINTH

The lively exchange of news and letters between
Paul and his Christian friends at Corinth is one of the
most fascinating subjects in the life of the apostle.
I Corinthians was written near the close of his stay at
Ephesus, for he writes in I Cor. 16:8, "I will tarry at
Ephesus until Pentecost." But this was not his first
communication. In I Cor. 5:9 are the words, "I wrote
unto you in my epistle," indicating that he had written
them a previous letter, of which unfortunately only a
fragment is now extant. But this is not all. The
Corinthians had written a letter to Paul, to which he
refers in 7:1: "Now concerning the things whereof ye
wrote."

Moreover, Paul had repeatedly received verbal reports of the progress of his Corinthian converts. We have the names of several who brought him news. On one occasion it was the family of Chloe, mentioned in I Cor. 1:11. On another occasion it was Stephanas (I Cor. 16:15 and 1:16), the "firstfruits of Achaia," whom Paul had himself baptized. Stephanas had brought with him Fortunatus and Achaicus, by whom the church had apparently sent Paul a special gift, for which he expresses his gratitude in I Cor. 16:17.

But the relation of church and apostle was not limited to reports and letters. At some time during his stay in Ephesus Paul had himself paid a visit to Corinth, for he writes in II Cor. 12:14 and 13:1: "This is the third time I am coming to you." Again, he had sent Timothy to them. I Cor. 4:17 and 16:10 perhaps mean that he had sent him on two different occasions. Titus, too, had been sent and had brought back comforting news when Paul wrote II Cor. 7:6.

The reasons for this lively intercourse are to be found partly in the proximity of Corinth to Ephesus, partly also in the peculiar affection which Paul felt for the church where he had spent so long a time, but principally in a great crisis which was developing in the attitude of the church toward Paul. It became, next to the Galatian crisis, the greatest in Paul's career. Yet the apostle's firmness and gentleness won him the victory at last.

The history of the difficulties in the Corinthian church, although passed over in silence by Luke, can be quite fully reconstructed from Paul's letters.

1. In I Cor. 5:9–11 we have a description of Paul's previous letter. It was concerned mainly with the

question of whether the Christian converts might associate with immoral persons. This letter the Corinthians misunderstood. They interpreted it as meaning that Christians should not associate with unconverted sinners. In I Cor. 5:11 he explains that his meaning was that Christians should not tolerate the presence of an immoral Christian in their own ranks. Now it is a remarkable fact that II Cor. 6:14—7:1 is a passage on exactly this subject and capable of precisely the same misinterpretation. It is further quite noticeable that the thought broken off in 6:13 is picked up and continued in 7:2. It is possible and probable that this passage is a page out of the letter in question. How it came to be preserved in II Corinthians will be explained later in connection with that letter.

2. In response to Paul's brief note the Corinthians wrote a somewhat extended letter asking questions of various kinds about their Christian life and religious services (I Cor. 7:1). It included questions about marriage, about eating things that had been offered in· idol sacrifices, the conduct of women in Christian meetings, the proper way to observe the Lord's Supper, the relative value of the various "gifts of the spirit," and perhaps included finally questions about the resurrection. At about the same time with the arrival of this letter of questions came the news brought by the family of Chloe (I Cor. 1:11) that the Corinthian church had split up into several factions.

3. In reply Paul wrote the letter called I Corinthians, a letter which must have seemed to Paul at the time an extremely long and elaborate one. It shows the great versatility of the man that he could in the same letter

write six chapters of reproach and two passages of such extraordinary beauty as chapters 13 and 15.

The first four chapters of I Corinthians have to do with the factions. It is easy to understand what had happened. When Apollos after leaving Ephesus (Acts 18:27) arrived at Corinth his unusual ability in the use of Scripture, probably both by the citation of prophecy and by allegorical interpretation, soon became known. "Greeks seek after wisdom," as Paul says in I Cor. 1:22. The learning and eloquence and public power of Apollos pleased the Corinthians. Soon the cry arose on the part of some that he was greater than Paul. His "wisdom" from the Greek point of view perhaps did exceed Paul's. Any student of Greek history knows the Greek tendency to party spirit. Although Apollos apparently refused to lead his faction and was back again in Ephesus with Paul when he wrote I Cor. 16:12, the division in the church grew steadily more bitter and hostile.

There not unnaturally appeared also in Corinth a party which followed the lead of the head apostles at Jerusalem, and especially of Peter. That Peter had been in Corinth is doubtful. But that his controversy with Paul at Antioch became known is quite certain. This party at Corinth was probably composed largely of Jews and Jewish proselytes, who held to the general observance of the law by Jews.

Was there a fourth party? In I Cor. 3:22 Paul mentions only three, "Whether Paul or Apollos or Cephas." In 1:12 he mentions four, "Each of you saith, I am of Paul, and I of Apollos, and I of Cephas, and I of Christ." It is possible that those who said "I of Christ" were only a conciliatory group who were trying to unify the church.

But it is far more likely that there was a fourth party led by certain ones who based their claims upon personal relation to or acquaintance with Jesus. In fact it seems to have been this Christ party which later headed the whole opposition to Paul (II Cor. 10:7; 11:23). That those who adopted this watchword "of Christ" were outsiders who came probably from Jerusalem is amply substantiated by the references to them in II Corinthians (10:7; 11:4, 13, 22, 23). In all probability they were Judaizers, who insisted on a general observance of the Jewish law by all Christians, both Jews and Gentiles, and made much of personal acquaintance with Jesus.

In answer to all this factious spirit Paul portrays the simple, unphilosophical character of the gospel of a crucified Christ, and appeals to the lowliness of his own preaching among them (1:10—3:4). Explaining that he and Apollos and others were only workmen engaged on God's one great work (3:5–17), he begs them in like manner to forsake wrangling and join in loyal support of the one who has spent so long a time with them in self-sacrificing service (3:18—4:16). He is sending Timothy and warns them that he may come himself very soon (4:17–21).

Leaving the subject of the factions, Paul in chapters 5 and 6 rebukes the immorality and general bad conduct which had been reported to him. He mentions especially the case of a man who had married his stepmother (chap. 5). This was forbidden both by Jewish and Roman law. In this case we may perhaps infer from the severity of Paul's rebuke that the father, though absent, was still living.

In chapter 7 he turns to the questions contained in the letter from Corinth. The first question concerned marriage. In general Paul seems to exalt celibacy above wedlock. It is hardly necessary to say that any advice against marrying was not unrelated to his expectation of Christ's speedy coming. His words concerning personal chastity must have been of great effect in sanctifying the marriage vow and in giving to women, both married and unmarried, the respect which was so sadly lacking in the profligate city of Corinth.

In chapters 8–10 he takes up their questions about eating things sacrificed to idols. Paul answers that Christian liberty allows eating of such things (chap. 8), but points to the fact that he himself does not take advantage of his apostolic liberty (chap. 9). Therefore the Corinthian Christians should be guided, not by what is permissible, but by what is of most help to others (chap. 10).

Chapters 11–14 concern subjects connected with their Christian meetings. In 11: 2–16 he expresses regret that certain Corinthian women had so far reveled in their Christian liberty that they had discarded the usual customs of decent headdress and modest behavior. In reproving the practice of praying and prophesying in public without a veil, he says that since there is "no such custom" neither should "the churches of God" adopt such questionable procedure. In the same connection he rebukes their disorder at the Lord's Supper (11: 17–34).

Chapter 12, dealing with various spiritual gifts, reflects the ecstatic condition into which Christians in their enthusiasm over possession of the spirit were

sometimes carried. Speaking with tongues was apparently practiced at Corinth in a way that was not far
different from the ramblings of a Greek prophetess of
Apollo in her uttering of oracles.   Paul ranks such unin-
telligent speaking with tongues as the least of spiritual
gifts (vs. 28).   Over against his list of the *gifts* of the
Spirit which he here depreciates should be set his list
of the *fruits* of the Spirit which he elsewhere so highly
exalts—love, joy, peace, longsuffering, kindness, goodness, faithfulness, meekness, self-control (Gal. 5:22 f.).
To this "most excellent way" he devotes that marvelous
little poem (chap. 13) on the first of the fruits of the
Spirit:

> And if I have the gift of preaching
> And have all wisdom and knowledge . . . .
> And have not love
> I am nothing.

In chapter 14, resuming the subject of spiritual gifts,
he exalts prophecy, i.e., intelligible Christian exhortation or preaching, far above speaking with tongues
(14:1–25).   He lays down the principle that all who take
part in meeting should speak, not for their own edification, but for the edification of all present (14:26–40).

Finally in chapter 15 he answers doubts concerning
the resurrection, explaining the nature of the resurrection body, and closing with a masterful picture of the
glory of the resurrection.   He adds a postscript in
chapter 16 concerning the collection for Jerusalem, and
sends greeting from "the churches of Asia," and especially from Aquila and Priscilla.

4. In reading through II Corinthians every thoughtful inquirer is struck by a significant diversity of tone.

In chapters 1–9 Paul consistently speaks of the situation in Corinth as highly pleasing and satisfactory. In chapter 7 especially he speaks of the great relief and comfort brought by Titus and his good news. In verse 9 he writes: "I now rejoice not that ye were made sorry but that ye were made sorry unto repentance." And again, "What earnest care is wrought in you? . . . . In everything ye have proved yourselves to be pure in the matter . . . . therefore we have been comforted. . . . . Titus . . . . remembereth the obedience of you all. . . . . I rejoice that in everything I am of good courage concerning you."

On the other hand chapters 10–13 are full of strong invective. They tingle with indignation and denunciation. The more one studies these chapters the more he is convinced that they were not written at the same time with the earlier chapters. It would appear that these chapters 10–13 belong to another letter and were placed where they are by a later copyist or collector of Paul's correspondence. With this possibility in mind, after reading Paul's words in II Cor. 7:16, "I rejoice that in everything I am of good courage concerning you," read the righteous anger and cutting sarcasm of this other letter.

I beseech you that I may not when present show courage with the confidence wherewith I count to be bold against some. . . . . For his letters they say are weighty and strong, but his bodily presence is weak and his speech of no account. Let such a one reckon this, that what we are in words by letter when we are absent such are we also in deed when we are present. . . . . Even Satan fashioneth himself into an angel of light. . . . . Are they Hebrews? So am I. . . . . At the mouth of two witnesses or three shall every word be established. . . . . I say plainly as when I was present the second time that if I come again I will not spare . . . . for this cause I write these things while absent that I may not when present deal sharply according to the authority which the Lord gave me.

This denunciatory letter affords deep insight into the personal power of Paul and into the critical nature of the battle which he had to fight out at Corinth. But when was it written? Indications are quite definite that it was written before the letter contained in the first chapters of II Corinthians. Three of these indications are as follows:

a) In II Cor. 2:4 Paul states, "Out of much affliction and anguish of heart I wrote unto you with many tears." The letter to which he here refers must have been just such a sharp, intense denunciation of his enemies as II Cor., chaps. 10–13. He makes several other references in II Cor., chaps. 1–7, to this previous letter, even indicating that at one time he was sorry he had sent it. "Though I made you sorry with my epistle, I do not regret it though I did regret it" (II Cor. 7:8).

b) Another indication of this previous letter may be found in the fact that the offender mentioned in II Cor. 2:5–11 and 7:12 cannot be identified with the offender rebuked in I Cor., chap. 5. Yet Paul says plainly in 2:9 and elsewhere that he had written a letter concerning this later offender. It is quite evident from 2:5, 8; 7:12 that the offender was one who had personally insulted and opposed Paul.

c) Finally, still another hint of the letter is found in the fact that Paul sent Timothy at the time he wrote I Corinthians, mentioning him in 4:17 and 16:10. But in II Cor. 7:6 and elsewhere it is Titus, not Timothy, who has returned from Corinth and brought back news to Paul. Evidently Titus had been the bearer of the letter in question.

II Corinthians is thus not one letter but a collection of letters or parts of letters. As suggested in another chapter of this volume, Paul's followers after his death evidently began to think seriously of the matter of collecting his letters as far as they were still in existence. Many churches would not have preserved all that they received. A study of Philippians reveals reference to several letters which that church must have lost in whole or in part. Some churches preserved all of certain letters and only parts of others. Apparently one of Paul's disciples, going around after the death of the apostle with the object of making a collection, and coming to Corinth, found one long letter which would just about fill a standard papyrus roll. After copying the letter he would number this roll Corinthians I. Then using a second roll of papyrus he arranged the shorter letters or fragments as best he could, copied them, and numbered the roll Corinthians II.

In this second roll of Corinthian correspondence were probably to be found parts or all of four or five letters. It was noted above that 6:14—7:1 belongs to a letter written before I Corinthians, advising a separatist policy toward immoral Christians. Chapters 10–13 are from a letter of severe reproof which Paul sent some time after I Corinthians in an effort to foil a party of outsiders who were heading up the whole opposition and stealing away his church. Chapters 1–7, with the exception of the paragraph noted above, are an expression of Paul's gratitude and relief that all has gone well and that the crisis is over. This was written from Macedonia upon the arrival of Titus (2:12, 13; 7:5). There are left only chapters 8 and 9, which deal with the collection for the saints. These two chapters can hardly have been written at the same time, for 9:1 introduces the subject in a way that indicates it had not been mentioned before. Both pleas for the collection may have been sent from Macedonia (8:1; 9:2), and not far apart in time, since both speak of Achaia as having made a preliminary contribution one year previously (8:10; 9:2).

The correspondence of Paul with his Corinthian Christians may be summarized as follows:

1. Paul's separatist letter to the Corinthians (II Cor. 6:14—7:1). Mentioned in I Cor. 5:9. Written from Ephesus perhaps in the year 54.

2. The letter of the Corinthians to Paul. Mentioned in I Cor. 7:1. Written early in 55. Contained questions about marriage, eating things sacrificed to idols, etc.

3. Paul's reply—our I Corinthians. Written at Ephesus in the spring of 55, as indicated by 16:8. Rebukes the four factions and answers the questions of the Corinthians.

4. Paul's letter of stern reproof to the Corinthians (II Cor., chaps. 10–13). Mentioned in II Cor. 2:4, 9; 7:8. Written about the time of leaving Ephesus, Pentecost 55.

5. The letter of reconciliation (II Cor. 1:1—6:13; 7:2–16). Written in Macedonia (II Cor. 7:5) in the summer of 55.

6. Two brief letters concerning the collection (II Cor., chaps. 8 and 9). One or both perhaps written in Macedonia in 55.

2. THROUGH MACEDONIA TO CORINTH

Paul had previously planned to go from Ephesus by boat across to Corinth and later to revisit the churches of Macedonia.   This plan, mentioned in II Cor. 1:16, was rendered impracticable by the increased acuteness of the dissension in the Corinthian church.   Paul considered it wiser to write the letter of stern reproof.   This he sent by the hand of Titus (II Cor. 7:6–8), who had already made a previous trip to Corinth, probably in connection with the collection for the saints (II Cor. 12:18).   It was in great uneasiness of mind that Paul then proceeded northward toward Macedonia.   When he reached Troas and found Titus had not yet returned he began to fear that the church had failed to respond to his appeal (II Cor. 2:12, 13; 7:6).   Momentarily he even regretted having sent such a sharp denunciation (7:8).

Upon his arrival in Macedonia he received the good news from Titus that the Corinthian church had been brought around to a firm stand of loyalty and comparative harmony.   Paul's good spirits revived.   After writing an expression of his joy to the Corinthians he went through the cities of Macedonia, not only giving his Christian friends the longed-for opportunity of seeing his face again but also imparting to them "much exhortation" and encouragement.

Although Luke makes no mention at this point of the collection for the saints, Paul's own references in his epistles suggest that this was one of the chief reasons for this tour of Macedonia.   The two letters, II Cor., chaps. 8 and 9, written at about this time, reflect the importance of the matter in the apostle's mind.   It is possible that this broad collection grew out of the original plea made years before by the apostles at the Jerusalem council that Paul remember the poor (Gal. 2:10). His purpose in making the collection, however, was not simply to relieve suffering, but in large measure also to bind the gentile and Jewish Christians together in one community. One of Paul's greatest and most frequent points of emphasis was the unity of all believers and all nations in Christ. Paul loved his nation, the Jews; he also had a large world-view. He could not face the thought of a separation. Rather he devoted his life to interpreting Jew to Gentile and Gentile to Jew. It was of utmost importance, then, that all his churches should participate in this unifying act of brotherly sympathy.

It is no mere accident that Paul in one place or another mentions all his churches as taking part. (1) In I Cor. 16:1 he speaks of the churches of Galatia. Perhaps Timothy carried the Galatian collection, since his home was in Galatia. (2) In Macedonia the man who had been appointed to take charge of contributions is mentioned in II Cor. 8:19. Paul writes of the collection in Macedonia also in Rom. 15:26. In II Cor. 8:2, 3 he praises the generosity of the Macedonians who gave "beyond their power." (3) The collection in Achaia, especially in Corinth, is mentioned in Rom. 15:26; I Cor. 16:1, 2; II Cor. 9:2. That Titus had charge of the collections there is shown by Paul's reference in II Cor. 8:6. (4) Although money from Ephesus is not distinctly mentioned, the collection was evidently the reason for the presence of Trophimus the Ephesian at Jerusalem, narrated in Acts 21:29. Only Cyprus is omitted. But Paul had left that to Barnabas.

This collection was not only the chief mission of Paul in Macedonia but also the chief occasion of Paul's journey to Jerusalem. Slanderous remarks of Paul's enemies implied that Paul was getting selfish gain in some way out of it; hence Paul's extreme care in not handling the money himself. I Cor. 16:2 states that he even preferred not to have the collection made while he was present. I Cor. 16:3 shows that he would not touch the money with his own hands. He felt that his journey to Jerusalem as head of a delegation bringing funds from all his churches would heal any wounds which his independence of other Christian apostles had caused at Jerusalem and would at the same time portray vividly to the Jewish Christians there the union and loyalty of all the Christian groups in the one great world-brotherhood.

After completing the collection in Macedonia he departed for one last, long visit in Corinth. I Cor. 16:6 states that he hoped to spend the winter there. Luke's statement that he spent three months in Greece agrees with this. During that winter, the winter of 55–56, he lived at the home of his old friend Gaius, of whom he wrote in Rom. 16:23. This was the same Gaius whom he mentioned in I Cor. 1:14 as one of those whom he had personally baptized. His winter's stay must have been full of earnest yet joyful and satisfying work amid the reunited Christian brotherhood.

3. THE EPISTLE TO THE ROMANS

During the winter at Corinth Paul's desire to see Rome naturally increased. Ships were departing constantly from Corinth for the world-capital. At times perhaps, from the lofty summit of Acro-Corinthus, he looked out over the gulf toward the west and thought of possibilities for the gospel in that direction even to the end of the Great Sea at the shores of Spain (15:24, 28). But then turning around he would gaze into the distance toward the other end of the Mediterranean and think of the Christian community at Jerusalem and of the elaborate collection which he had gathered (15:25, 31).

The latter half of the fifteenth chapter of Romans reveals the magnitude of some of Paul's plans The journey of which he speaks so simply—from Corinth to Jerusalem and back to Rome and to Spain—was a journey of at least four thousand miles. If he afterward returned to his home or to Antioch the minimum total would be nearly seven thousand miles. Considering the slowness of travel in the Roman Empire, the trip was more elaborate and extended than a twentieth-century one around the world.

Giving up the idea of even hastily visiting Rome in the near future, he did the next best thing. He procured a letter writer, and in his room in the house of Gaius, dictating probably a few hours each morning before his day's work, he wrote a long letter to the Christians in the Imperial City. He explained that he had been hoping "these many years" to come to them, that he had, however, just taken up the collection in Macedonia and Achaia, that he must first proceed with this to Jerusalem before going westward. The importance which he attached to the collection and his concern that the Roman Christians should at least in spirit have a share in it are reflected in his request for their prayers that it might be "acceptable" at Jerusalem.

His reason for writing lay partly in the fact that he was so near Rome, partly also in his fear that the Roman church would perhaps in the meantime before his arrival be influenced toward a Judaistic conception of the gospel message, mainly, however, in his farsighted judgment that he might not be "delivered from them that are disobedient in Judea." In case he should never reach Rome he wished the Christians there to have a clear statement of his gospel of spiritual freedom.

In his first chapters he portrays the universality of sin and guilt. Neither among the Gentiles without law (chap. 1) nor among the Jews who possessed the law (2:1—3:20) had men been able to achieve "salvation" by their own merits. Beginning with 3:21 and continuing to the end of the first eight chapters he describes the new way of righteousness revealed by Jesus. In chapter 7 he narrates his own personal struggle with sin, and in chapter 8 the victory which he finally gained and all other men may gain through the spirit of Christ. "The good which I would I do not: but the evil which I would not that I practice. . . . . The spirit of life in Christ Jesus made me free from the law of sin and of death." Chapters 9–11 take up the question of the future destiny of God's chosen people who have rejected Jesus. He utters the earnest hope, even the confident conviction, that they will turn and be received into the Kingdom upon the same basis as the Gentiles. Finally in chapters 12–15 he gives a practical application of the spirit of Christ to the lives of the Christians at Rome.

The Epistle to the Romans is the least personal of Paul's letters. It should perhaps be called a treatise rather than a letter. Yet it is an expression of Paul's inner soul. In chapter 7 he relates his early battles with himself. In chapter 9 he cries out that he would be glad to be lost himself if his nation could be saved. In chapter 15 he reveals the largest ambitions of his life. Thus there are embodied in the letter three elements of Paul's personal greatness, the depth and purity of his soul, his absolute devotion to the welfare of his fellow-men, the vastness of his plans.

Romans ends with the benediction and with the "Amen" at the close of chapter 15. Chapter 16 is a short letter of recommendation which in the later collecting was copied on the same roll with the long letter. It must have been written to some church which Paul could call his own, for in verse 19 he says, "I rejoice over you." Its probable destination appears as soon as one begins to read it. Priscilla and Aquila were, so far as we know, still in Ephesus. Hence the note containing the salutation to them was in all probability addressed to that city. The next salutation is to Epaenetus, who is identified as a probable Ephesian by the phrase "the firstfruits of Asia." Two verses later Paul salutes his "fellow-prisoners," men whose acquaintance he doubtless had made during the probable imprisonment at Ephesus.

Nowhere else in the letters is there such a profusion of salutations. Paul remembered so many friends who had stood by him in those three years at Ephesus that he can hardly limit the number of names. The little note affords an unusual insight into the friendships which Paul formed wherever he went. Think of that good woman in Ephesus who had taken such patient,

affectionate care of Paul in that strange city that he had
become accustomed to call her "mother" (vs. 13).

4. FROM CORINTH TO JERUSALEM

Paul's plan to sail directly from Corinth to the east
was changed because of the threatening attitude of the
Jews, who intended to do away with him if possible by
fair means or foul.   The double visitation of Macedonia
he had before at Ephesus planned to avoid by sailing
from Ephesus to Corinth and thence to Macedonia.
Now as then his plan was changed, and he proceeded
through Macedonia a second time.   On the way the
seven men who accompanied him, probably as official
carriers of contributions from the churches, left him at
Philippi with Luke and went on ahead to Troas.   These
men may have traveled with Paul from Troas all the
way to Jerusalem.   The words "as far as Asia" were
almost certainly not a part of the original text of Acts
20:4.   In fact two of the men are later mentioned by
name with Paul in Palestine.

The sudden reappearance of the pronoun "we" in
20:5 is full of significance.   Paul's retinue of delegates
was accompanying "him" (20:4).   But at Philippi it
is "we" who sailed away.   And the delegates, going on
ahead to Troas, were waiting for "us."   Three suggestions may be found in the narrative with more or less
clearness: (1) That Luke probably joined Paul at
Philippi to make the journey with him to Jerusalem.
(2) That possibly Luke's decision to accompany Paul
was in some way connected with the delay which made
it necessary for the delegation to wait at Troas for "us."
Could it have been that Luke was not expecting to go and

that if Paul had sailed directly from Corinth he might
have missed his physician companion and the Christian
world might have missed the Book of Acts? (3) In any
case Luke now begins to make use of extracts from his
diary. The pronoun "we" continues, with the exception of the Caesarean imprisonment, through most of
the rest of the narrative portion of the Acts (20:5–15;
21:1–18; 27:1—28:16). That original daily record of
travel Luke apparently wrote so regularly that he preserved names of even little unimportant stops which
the vessel made, such as the touching at Samos
(20:15).

One of the incidents recorded by Luke in his journal
was that of the young man at Troas who became sleepy
when Paul talked too long. Perhaps even to his grand-
children on his knees Luke narrated how Paul "prolonged his speech until midnight" and how "as Paul
discoursed yet longer" the lad was borne down with
"deep sleep." But the story had its serious side, for
the lad was apparently killed by his fall from the window.
Although Luke was a physician, he seems to say (vs. 9)
that the boy was dead, and implies that Paul restored him
to life in the same manner as Elijah restored the widow's
son in I Kings 17:21.

From Troas Paul went by land as far as Assos, about
twenty miles, and there rejoined his ship. The frequent
stopping of the vessel, which was of course largely for
loading and unloading of freight, is paralleled to a considerable extent in the case of modern steamers. For
example, nearly every steamer which stops at Smyrna
remains long enough for a tourist to make the trip to the
ruins of Ephesus and back to Smyrna. Similarly in

Paul's day at Miletus, although he could not tell exactly when his "steamer" might sail, and so would not wish to leave the vicinity, he still had time to send for the elders at Ephesus for a parting word with them.

Paul's reason for choosing a ship which sailed past Ephesus without stopping lay no doubt partly in the thought that his reappearance at Ephesus so soon after his stormy departure would occasion trouble, but principally in the fact that the unexpected second trip through Macedonia had delayed him considerably. He was very anxious to be in Jerusalem at Pentecost. This day was not only a great Jewish celebration, but an anniversary of the outpouring of the Spirit described in Acts, chap. 2. It would be a particularly opportune and appropriate occasion for presenting the contribution of the gentile churches to the Jewish Christians.

The farewell at Miletus perhaps served Paul's purpose better than a visit to Ephesus. His principal wish was that his disciples there should remain true to him and his teaching. They would understand after these words that any fate which might overtake him at Jerusalem did not mean his defeat, but the unflinching completion of his purpose. If "they should behold his face no more," they could not help remembering his personal work and his self-sacrificing devotion in their behalf. His closing words preserve a saying of Jesus nowhere else recorded: "It is more blessed to give than to receive."

When Paul and his friends on their eastward voyage sailed past Cyprus, Paul perhaps pointed out to Luke the mountains of that island, describing his missionary campaign with Barnabas. Ever afterward those words "sight of Cyprus" in Luke's diary would remind him of the beginning and the end of Paul's missionary journeys.

Arrived at Tyre the company had to wait seven days for a ship in which to continue the voyage. Paul was warned that Jewish antagonism had mounted high against him. But again he set his face steadfastly to go up to Jerusalem, as Jesus had done before him. The voyage ended at Ptolemais, and the rest of the trip was to be made by land. After stopping only overnight the travelers on the next day came as far as Caesarea. Here at the place where Paul was soon afterward to spend two years in prison he received his final warning. The nearer he came to Jerusalem the more clearly his Christian comrades told him of the danger ahead. He did not waver. After a few days the journey up the slope toward Jerusalem was begun. Although the road had been well paved by the Romans, the distance was somewhat long for a single day's ride. The night was passed at the home of an early disciple from Cyprus named Mnason. The word "early" is a hint that he had been converted by Paul on that first journey. Here again the beginning and the end came close together. Paul could narrate to his host the general course of all that had happened since he left the island. The next morning, continuing the journey, the company arrived at Jerusalem, probably only a few days before Pentecost.

SUPPLEMENTARY READING

1. Foakes-Jackson, *Saint Paul*, pp. 180–203.
2. McNeile, A. H., *St. Paul*, pp. 86–95, 135–68; 181–203.
3. Wood, C. T., *Life of Paul*, pp. 159–277.
4. Ramsay, *St. Paul the Traveller*, pp. 283–303.
5. Kent, *Work and Teachings of the Apostles*, pp. 151–55; 185–90.

6. Gilbert, *Student's Life of Paul*, pp. 157–74.
7. Conybeare and Howson, *Life and Epistles of St. Paul*, chaps. xvii–xx.
8. Farrar, *Life and Work of St. Paul*, chap. xxxiv.
9. *Bible for Home and School*, "Acts," pp. 187–200.
10. McGiffert, *A History of Christianity in the Apostolic Age*, pp. 290–337.
11. Cone, *Paul*, pp. 107–27; 138–42.
12. Bacon, *The Story of St. Paul*, 182–85; 266–97.

ON THE CORINTHIAN LETTERS AND ROMANS

13. Burton, *Handbook of the Life of the Apostle Paul*, pp. 59–78.
14. Goodspeed, *Story of the New Testament*, pp. 14–34.
15. Moffatt, *Introduction to the New Testament*, pp. 108–49.

CHAPTER XI

ARREST AND APPEAL

I. ARREST AT JERUSALEM

To understand the incidents narrated in Acts, chaps. 21–25, it is necessary to have clearly in mind the various factors in the situation and the attitude of each toward Paul and his Jerusalem visit. The principal factors were six: (1) Paul himself, (2) the Jerusalem apostles, (3) the legalistic element in the Christian community at Jerusalem, (4) the non-Christian Jews, (5) the gentile Christians, (6) the Roman authorities.

1. Paul's object in making this Jerusalem visit was, as stated before, to preserve and establish the unity of Christendom, no matter what might be the hazard or the cost to him personally. His fear was that Christianity would be divided into a Jewish Christian body that would be more Jewish than Christian and a gentile Christian body that would lack the strength that would come from close connection with the Old Testament religion and with the personal disciples of Jesus. Each

branch of the church needed the other, and Paul was determined if possible to keep them together. This was the purpose of the collection and of his insistence upon carrying it to Jerusalem himself. Of course Paul was also determined that in maintaining this union the Gentiles should not be subjected to Judaistic legalism. But that point did not come up on this visit. That had been settled by the previous Jerusalem conference and by the Antiochian, Galatian, and Corinthian controversies. The purifying of the four men that had a vow (Acts 21:24), as will be seen later, had nothing to do with the freedom of Gentiles from all such ceremonies. This visit was solely in the interest of promoting a practical brotherly unity of all believers, Jew and Gentile, in Christ.

2. The pillar apostles represented by James (21:18) were apparently in entire sympathy with Paul's gentile mission in general and with his purpose on this visit in particular. When Paul, as Luke says, "rehearsed one by one the things which God had wrought among the Gentiles," they "glorified God." James was apparently quite willing to welcome the conversion of Gentiles on a non-legalistic basis. But there was another element in the church with which he had to reckon.

3. The legalists in the Jerusalem church made the situation a three-cornered one, as was the case in the earlier Jerusalem conference (Gal., chap. 2; Acts, chap. 15). The question raised this time was not the circumcision of Gentiles but Paul's attitude toward the observance of the law by Jews. Possibly these legalists were so numerous and at the same time so suspicious of Paul that they held back the church from a hearty

response to the handing over of the collection. Luke has nothing to say concerning the receiving of the money or concerning any expression of thanks to the Gentiles. Perhaps Paul's fear that his ministration might not be "acceptable" (Rom. 15:30, 31) proved to have real ground.

The pillar apostles wishing to assist him in his purpose of cementing friendship between Jew and Gentile made a proposition that he should conciliate the legalists by assisting in the purifying of four Jews who were perhaps too poor to carry out all the ceremonies themselves. In one respect this proposition paralleled the request made years before that Paul circumcise Titus, in that both were based, not on the conviction of the apostles themselves, but upon the scruples of the legalists in the church (cf. Gal. 2:1–10). The pillar apostles wished Paul to give assurance that the acceptance of the Gentiles on a non-legalistic basis did not mean that he was encouraging disregard of the law on the part of Jewish Christians (Acts 21:21).

This request was one with which Paul could comply. So far as we know he never undertook any program of dissuading Jews from observance of their law. While it was doubtless true that these legalists were more Jewish than Christian, yet they were members of the Christian community and therefore came within Paul's purpose of conciliation and unification. So he consented to take a share in the purifying rites. The last part of verse 24, "that thou thyself also walkest orderly, keeping the law," in Luke's report of what James said cannot have been based upon a profession on Paul's part that he always on all occasions kept the law. For he had reproved Peter at Antioch for observing legal scruples at the expense of Christian brotherhood. Verse 25 also, referring to the restrictions placed upon the Gentiles, should be read in the light of what has been said concerning these "decrees" in connection with the Antioch incident. They were undoubtedly restrictions placed only upon Gentiles in Judea and in localities where Jews predominated. With these modifications of the narrative we may conclude that Paul willingly undertook to follow the conciliatory suggestion of the apostles. But this well-meant and well-received proposition led to a serious clash with the non-Christian Jews.

4. The Jews outside the Christian circle would perhaps have found no special occasion for inciting feeling against Paul had they not found him in the Temple. The general attitude of the Jews, however, toward Paul's gentile preaching was one of intense hostility. Their view was that in the great cities of the empire he was stealing away many Jews and a host of the "fearers of God" from the synagogues of the Dispersion, proclaiming that men may be saved apart from the law. From the point of view of the Dispersion he was founding a rival religion which was undermining their work of winning Gentiles to the worship of Jehovah. It was natural that the Jerusalem outbreak should be led by Jews of Asia, the province in which Paul had recently been spending three years of active preaching. These men roused the Jews of Jerusalem by saying that Paul had brought with him into the Temple Trophimus, a gentile Christian of Ephesus.

5. Gentile Christians were not so specifically objects of hatred by the Jews as Paul was. Paul was regarded

as having turned against his own national religion. Toward gentile Christians in general the attitude among the Dispersion seems to have been mainly one of "jealousy" (Acts 17:5). There are hints of persecution of Christians by Jews (I Thess. 2:14) and of an intense feeling that if the Christians were right the Jews must be lost (Phil. 1:28). But it was not so much the sight of Trophimus in Jerusalem which angered the Jews as the presence in the Temple of him whom they considered the archenemy of the Temple and its elaborate worship, and who had forfeited his native rights in relation to it.

6. The Roman authorities had two reasons for according Paul just and liberal treatment. On the one side the government had a well-established and far-reaching policy of toleration toward all religions. The Jews had been especially privileged in this regard. Moreover, Paul was himself born a Roman citizen and as such was immune from all local persecution, having a right to claim the protection of Roman officials in any case of necessity. In the Book of Acts Luke takes special interest in narrating cases in which Paul and his fellow-Christians were vindicated, portraying the attitude of the government as constantly and consistently friendly.

The excitement and the outbreak in the Temple, directed primarily against Paul, centered around the accusation that he had brought Trophimus, a Gentile, into the inner court. The notice warning foreigners against entering was discovered some years ago and is now in the museum in Constantinople. There are copies of it in various American museums (e.g., Haskell).

The stone is about two feet high by three feet in width. The inscription reads as follows:

> No foreigner may
> Enter within the railing
> Or boundary line of the
> Sanctuary. Whoever is
> Caught is himself responsible
> For the consequences
> Which are death.

It is not impossible that some of the scars upon this block were made by Roman battle-axes. Mommsen in his *Roman History* writes that if the marks are those of an ax undoubtedly they were inflicted by the soldiers of Titus at the sack of the city in 70 A.D. If the soldiers did seek to vent their anger upon it they found it rugged and solid like the Jewish religion itself. The stone measures over a foot in thickness.

The Roman guard saved Paul from suffering such a fate as befell Stephen. This guard had become particularly watchful in these last years of the Jewish state. Stationed in the tower of Antonia at the corner of the Temple area, the soldiers heard immediately any disturbance which might arise. In this case Lysias was especially quick in acting because in the suppression of a recent uprising the leader, who was known as "the Egyptian," had apparently escaped (Acts 21:38). Instead of a Jewish fanatical insurrectionist, Lysias found a man who could address him in the Greek language, not a native of Palestine, but a "citizen of no mean city." He at once consented to Paul's request to be allowed to address the people.

Paul's words ought to have impressed the Jews by their evident sincerity if for no other reason. But the conversion experience which meant so much to him did not mean much to these excited and noisy antagonists. Representatives, not of the true spirit of Judaism, which found such noble and notable expression in the psalmists and prophets of the Old Testament, but of the perverted legalism of later times, itself akin in spirit to those who in the days of the prophets resisted and rejected their message, they failed to see in Paul a true successor of the prophets and conservator of the best traditions of the nation.

When Paul's speech failed to end the tumult, Lysias, who had perhaps not understood the Aramaic speech, commanded him to be examined under scourging in order to force a confession of whatever misdemeanor had so aroused the people. Then it was that Paul uttered those famous words, "But I am a Roman born."

All charges of a religious nature were brought to trial before the Sanhedrin. If the Sanhedrin had decided that Paul was worthy of death, the next step would have been to secure the consent of the Roman government to his execution. But by his skilful handling of the situation he escaped conviction by that council.

As he was beginning his defense the high priest, as Luke records (Acts 23:2), gave command to smite him on the mouth. While this seems incredible, it is not out of line with the statement of Josephus that this same Ananias a few years later came to a violent end at the hands of the Jews.

Paul had perhaps at one time been himself a member of the Sanhedrin (cf. Acts 26:10). He knew the nature of that body and the differences of view which existed.

By his words, "Brethren, I am a Pharisee," and by his reference to the resurrection of the dead (cf. Mark 12:18), he precipitated a division in the council between the Pharisees and the Sadducees. It is easy to see how in the dissension which followed, Lysias decided to remove the cause of the disturbance and to bring him back to the castle.

But the enemies of Paul were persistent. They rightly felt that if they did not succeed in doing away with Paul in Jerusalem, the center of Judaism, they would have much less chance of succeeding anywhere else. When the rioting failed, when the Sanhedrin council failed, their only recourse was to secret plotting. Such plots under oath were very common in the last years of Jerusalem. But Paul had many friends in the city. It is possible that Paul's sister's son was not a Christian, and therefore was the more easily able to learn about the plot and to bring the news of it to the Roman captain.

Lysias, impressed by the intensity of the hatred against Paul, decided that political expediency demanded his removal. He provided as elaborate protection as he would on ordinary occasions have given to a member of an official Roman delegation. Seventy cavalry and four hundred infantry set out secretly by night to escort him to the Roman governor of Judea residing at Caesarea.

2. TWO YEARS AT CAESAREA

Caesarea, which a hundred years before Paul's imprisonment had been an insignificant village, was rebuilt and beautified by Herod the Great. He named it after Caesar Augustus, erecting there a temple for the worship of the emperor. The roadway from Jerusalem to Caesarea, splendidly paved with huge blocks of stone, can still be traced down the mountain slopes. Caesarea became the Roman port of Jerusalem and after 6 A.D. the residence of the Roman governors of Judea. The great library of a later day, when Eusebius wrote here his history of Christianity, had perhaps already been started in the time of Paul.

Felix, the governor of Judea, was appointed in the year 52 by the emperor Claudius. He and his brother had been slaves in the family of Claudius at Rome. Tacitus says that even when ruling a province he did it "in the spirit of a slave." He was one of the least efficient of the governors of Judea. He accepted bribes wherever and whenever he could get them. When he found the Jews restless he deliberately took advantage of the situation by fomenting uprisings that he might execute whom he wished and confiscate their property for his own use.

The first wife of Felix was a daughter of Anthony and Cleopatra. His later wife, Drusilla, mentioned in Acts 24:24, a Jewess renowned for her beauty, had been alienated by Felix from her former husband. She died in the eruption of Vesuvius in 79.

At the hearing before Felix the professional lawyer Tertullus, without much regard for veracity, said those things which were calculated to appeal to such a governor. Paul's answer in its decisive refutation of the charges and its demand for justice apparently also made an impression. But it is not probable that Felix cared much about Paul's innocence of the charge. The two facts which saved Paul and gained for him some degree of freedom were (1) his Roman citizenship and (2) his reference to bringing alms and offerings.

1. Paul's confident bearing as a Roman citizen must have attracted the notice of Felix. Often prisoners who stood before him whined and pleaded after the manner of the papyrus records of the time. Here was a man of Tarsus who had had the courage to face a mob in the Temple at Jerusalem. He had exhibited the presence of mind and cleverness, while facing the death sentence before the Sanhedrin, calmly to precipitate a discussion about the resurrection and so avoid condemnation. He now stood before the Roman governor proudly and confidently as though he welcomed the chance to talk with the official about the new faith. Felix gave orders to show Paul "indulgence." The statement, "Felix was terrified," perhaps reflects a genuine inner respect which Felix conceived for this man and his message.

2. The reference in Acts 24:17 to the bringing of alms is the only mention of this subject in the Book of Acts. Its special significance in the ears of Felix is not hard to imagine. This man Paul, it appeared, had friends throughout the world who were willing to contribute money. We can understand at least one motive which prompted Felix to allow his "friends to minister unto him" (24:23), hoping that "money would be given him by Paul." How fine it would be to have a collection gathered in Macedonia and Achaia for the chief "saint" in the palace at Caesarea!

The two years which Paul spent in limited freedom at Caesarea were undoubtedly full of influence and activity. Luke was not with him, although the familiar pronoun "we" later reappears in Acts 27:1 at the departure from Caesarea. Perhaps Luke had sailed back to Macedonia after taking his part in delivering the collection at Jerusalem. Or possibly he made the acquaintance of apostles in Jerusalem and in Galilee and perhaps even at Antioch, inquiring concerning the life and deeds of Jesus. Perhaps he collected at this time some small part of the materials for writing his gospel. Paul, always active, would spend much time in consultation with the "friends" who came to visit him. Perhaps sometimes a Christian from Galatia or Asia made the trip to Caesarea in order to bring a gift or to take back a message from the apostle. Paul may have written some letters to his churches. We know that several of his epistles have been lost. And often during those two years he must have walked along the masonry of the castle above the breaking waves and have looked longingly westward toward his beloved churches in Asia and Macedonia and Achaia and toward the yet unvisited regions of Rome and of Spain.

3. APPEAL TO THE EMPEROR

Paul had waited long and hopefully for a change in the governorship. Any governor would be better than Felix. Paul probably expected what did actually happen. The emperor demanded the resignation of Felix. In fact it was only the intervention of his brother Pallas, who had become very wealthy and influential in Rome, which saved Felix from disgrace and banishment.

The date of the recall of Felix and the accession of Festus has been the subject of much discussion. Our reckoning, based on the Gallio inscription, would date Paul's arrival in Jerusalem in 56. This agrees incidentally with the statement of Paul in Acts 24:10 that Felix, appointed in 52, had at that time been "many years" in office. Paul's imprisonment lasted two years. The accession of Festus, then, probably occurred in 58 (see also Hastings, *Dictionary of the Bible*, art. "Chronology").

When Festus entered upon his duties as governor he found Paul's case pressing for attention. The Jews came down to Caesarea and presented their charges. As a new governor he felt that he must conciliate the Jews as far as possible. He was about to accede to their demands that Paul be taken back to Jerusalem when Paul uttered those potent words, "I appeal unto Caesar."

Paul had three reasons for his appeal to Rome. In the first place he had probably been secretly informed of the plots against him mentioned in Acts 25:3. Perhaps the information did not come this time from his sister's son, but from some one of the friends who were allowed to visit him regularly. In the second place he knew the danger of being brought to trial in Jerusalem. He knew the spirit and atmosphere of what proved to be the last years of that city. He knew the reports which were pouring into Jerusalem from the Jewish communities of the Dispersion throughout the Roman Empire that the new Christian faith was growing more popular than Judaism, winning away from the synagogues their prospective members and their prestige.

A third and important motive in Paul's appeal was his impatient desire to see Rome and to preach his gospel there. "These many years" he had wanted to see the

Imperial City. His very bonds he used as a means of reaching his greatest goal. And the plan which he laid out in his freedom was accomplished in his imprisonment.

The Caesar to whom Paul appealed was the emperor Nero. Nero's fame for everything except justice is well known. We cannot but think of what his predecessor Claudius or even Augustus would have done. Paul would undoubtedly have been brought to trial soon after reaching Rome and have been set at liberty on condition that he should not return to Judea. The early years of Nero's reign were not like the later ones, and Paul was accorded a considerable degree of fair treatment. Yet from the point of view of later knowledge of Nero the general prospect for Paul was not an auspicious one.

The next problem which confronted Festus was his official report to Rome concerning Paul. In this he decided to ask the advice of King Agrippa. Agrippa was a great-grandson of Herod the Great. His domain lay upon the other side of Jordan, stretching northward toward Damascus. Although Idumean in family, his sympathies were very broad and tolerant. He was in fact more of a Roman than a Jew. He ruled until thirty years after the destruction of the Jewish capital (*ca.* 50 to 100 A.D.).

It was a matter of social etiquette for Agrippa to visit the new governor, Festus. Since Agrippa was a kind of mediator between the Jews and the Romans, understanding the prejudices and the ideals of both, it was natural that Festus should take advantage of his visit to secure an opinion concerning Paul.

The defense before King Agrippa was a forceful appeal. Paul knew that Agrippa admired many of the Jewish ideals. He also knew his international and universal outlook. It is not at all impossible that Paul really made an attempt to win Agrippa to the support of his gospel (Acts 26:28). He certainly did succeed in making plain that his persecution was due solely to the narrow, national prejudice of the Jews against the preaching of a freer, international gospel.

In writing his report to Rome Festus probably followed the statement of Agrippa, "This man might have been set at liberty if he had not appealed unto Caesar," for both on the voyage and at Rome Paul was accorded a considerable degree of freedom.

4. THE VOYAGE AND SHIPWRECK

The account of the voyage from Caesarea is written in the first person, probably in much the same form as Luke noted it down day by day in his diary. It is the most detailed narrative of its length in the Book of Acts. The description is, in fact, unique in ancient literature for portraying the life of sailors on their long, hazardous trips without engines and without compass. Luke's notes would compare well with many a modern journal of an ocean voyage. Along with Luke, Paul had another companion, Aristarchus, the same comrade who was seized by the mob at Ephesus, whom Paul mentions also in Col. 4:10 as his "fellow-prisoner." The centurion, Julius, was apparently a man of good Roman qualities. It was an honor to belong to the "Augustan" band.

Because the strong winds came from the northeast, the usual route taken by westbound vessels from Egypt or Palestine lay at first northward along the coast to Asia Minor and then westward. After the stop at Sidon, where Julius allowed Paul to visit the Christian community, the ship made a short cut across the upper corner of the Mediterranean, keeping under the lee of the island of Cyprus. Reaching the coast at Myra, the centurion found a vessel which was bound directly for Italy. It had a cargo of wheat from Alexandria. Besides its cargo it carried of crew and passengers 276 men. On leaving Myra the wind made it easier and safer to head southwest toward Crete than to attempt to hold against the wind through the rocky islands of the Aegean.

The vessel, Luke thinks, ought to have spent the winter in the first sheltered harbor on the southern coast of Crete because the season was getting late for sailing. The Fast of the Day of Atonement, which marked the time when the days and nights were equal, had already gone by. Paul's advice against proceeding farther than Fair Havens was based upon long experience. "Three times I suffered shipwreck. A night and a day have I been in the deep" (II Cor. 11:25). But seldom has the voice of a prophet been heeded "when the south wind blew softly." They decided upon one more run to the next harbor.

For two weeks they saw neither sun by day nor stars by night. For two weeks they sailed closely reefed on a starboard tack, hoping against hope that the northeaster would not drive them on the coast of Africa. For two weeks the only calm in the tempest was Paul's reassuring way of saying "Fear not."

The beach where the ship struck on the island of Malta about sixty miles south of Sicily still bears the

name "St. Paul's Bay." It was not an especially
pleasant place to pass the winter. Luke's diary reflects
the rising spirits of the party when after three months
on the island they reached the beautiful Bay of Naples
and amid the glory of an Italian spring landed at Puteoli.
The welcome which the brethren here accorded to
Paul, whom they had most of them probably never seen,
and the warmth with which they "entreated" him to
tarry with them seven days give a suggestive picture of
the Christian brotherhood which was everywhere spreading through the Roman world. These Christians would
minister to his wants and listen eagerly as he rehearsed
the adventures of his last months and years. Then they
must have sent messengers on ahead to announce Paul's
arrival to the Christian circle at Rome; for Paul and his
party, setting out upon the 130-mile journey to the
Imperial City, were again rejoiced at finding that Christian delegates had come a third of the way to meet them.

SUPPLEMENTARY READING

1. Foakes-Jackson, *Saint Paul*, pp. 203–20.
2. McNeile, A. H., *St. Paul*, pp. 95–117.
3. Wood, C. T., *Life of Paul*, pp. 278–308.
4. Ramsay, *St. Paul the Traveller*, pp. 303–43.
5. Kent, *Work and Teachings of the Apostles*, pp. 205–9; 216–20.
6. Gilbert, *Student's Life of Paul*, pp. 175–215.
7. Conybeare and Howson, *Life and Epistles of St. Paul*, chaps. xxi–xxiii.
8. *Bible for Home and School*, "Acts," pp. 201–53.
9. McGiffert, *A History of Christianity in the Apostolic Age*, pp. 338–62.
10. Cone, *Paul the Man, the Missionary, and the Teacher*, pp. 135–38; 143–44.
11. Bacon, *The Story of St. Paul*, pp. 186–214.

CHAPTER XII

AT ROME

1. TWO YEARS IN ROME

The only incident which Luke mentions with any fulness in the account of Paul's two years in Rome was his meeting once and again with the non-Christian Jews. It was Paul's custom on arriving in a city to plead first with the Jews. And here where the Jewish colony was so strong he undoubtedly made very special effort to win them over to a receptive attitude toward Christianity. As these Jews had "neither received letters from Judea" nor any verbal report against Paul, he found at the first meeting some ground for hope of success. But the second meeting dispelled it. After winning only a few converts he turned to work among the Gentiles.

His conduct of himself before Festus and before Agrippa had, as stated, probably occasioned a favorable report of his case to Rome. Perhaps also the personal word of the centurion, who had been impressed by Paul's bearing during the voyage and shipwreck, helped to secure for him some measure of freedom. For two years, in his own hired dwelling, guarded only by a soldier, he probably had no small part in building up that church which afterward became the leading Christian community of the world.

The philosopher Seneca was living in Rome at this same time. Seneca and Paul were alike in that they both suffered violent death under Nero in the cause of righteousness. But while Seneca was the personal friend of Nero, Paul was the friend of the poor. To reform Nero turned out to be a hopeless task. But to bring the spirit of God into the homes and lives of the people was Paul's successful and fruitful work. Christians of the early centuries delighted in imagining that Paul and Seneca were acquainted with each other and that they wrote letters to each other. But the so-called correspondence of Paul and Seneca is certainly fictitious.

One who visits Rome today and travels mile after mile through the underground passages of the catacombs can easily picture the lively Christian activity of the thousands of converts who used these passages in the second and following centuries. Here upon the walls in hundreds of places they painted Old Testament stories, from the Garden of Eden to the adventure of Jonah and the fish. Beside them they painted the story of the birth of Jesus, the feeding of the multitude, the mystic symbol of the fish, and a host of others. It is all suggestive, too, of the nature of Paul's activity. It was hidden out of sight, but its extent and its ramifications were almost endless. The pictures which Paul painted of triumph

over sin, of the birth of a new life, of the giving of the
word to hungry souls, of Jesus Christ as the Son of God
and Savior of the world—these pictures must have
lighted up and beautified many of the long and dreary
stretches of human existence in the under world of Rome.

2. THE LETTER TO THE PHILIPPIANS

One privilege allowed Paul in his protracted imprisonment was the writing and receiving of letters. While he
could not visit his churches in Macedonia, or Asia, he
could send personal messages as well as special warnings
against perversions of the gospel. He could receive
back word as to the progress of his converts and perhaps
sometimes be pleasantly surprised by the arrival of a
gift of money or other token of loyalty.

One bountiful gift from the Philippians was very
much appreciated. The letter to the Philippians, in
which he thanks them for the gift, was written while in
"bonds" (1:13, 17). Most scholars hold that the reference is to the imprisonment in Rome (cf. 1:13 and 4:22).
As mentioned in a previous chapter, this was the fourth
gift received by Paul from Philippi. The first and
second are mentioned in Phil. 4:16; the third in II Cor.
11:9 (cf. Phil. 4:15). Upon the receipt of each of the
four gifts Paul had undoubtedly sent a note of thanks.
The present letter may have been a fifth letter, since
it is not primarily a letter of thanks. The fourth gift
had arrived long before. A severe illness of the bearer
of the gift had intervened. Epaphroditus had fallen
sick "nigh unto death" (2:27). This man had perhaps
been sent in the idea that he would stay indefinitely with
Paul as a sort of assistant. But it seemed best on

account of his illness that he should return home. Our Philippians is the testimonial which he took home with him.

Other indications of the interchange of news are not lacking. The Philippians had word, perhaps from Paul himself, that Epaphroditus had fallen sick. Then Epaphroditus had heard that they had heard of his illness. His anxiety over their anxiety is expressed in Phil. 2:26.

It is not impossible that our present Philippians contains portions of more than one of the several letters. The change of theme is very sudden in 3:2. The phrase, "finally, my brethren," is in the middle of the letter (3:1) as we now have it, and a similar phrase, "finally, brethren," occurs again in 4:8. Polycarp, writing to the Philippians (chap. 3) in the early part of the second century, refers to the "epistles" of Paul to the Philippians. While the plural in Greek did not universally designate separate letters, i.e., epistles, the natural understanding of the passage creates a probability that Polycarp had access to more than one.

After his greeting and expression of gratitude for their loyalty to the gospel (1:1-11), Paul gives the Philippians news about himself (1:12-26) and pleads with them to live worthily of Christ (1:27—2:18). He hopes to send Timothy to them and before long to come himself; at present he is sending Epaphroditus, whose illness has been very severe (2:19-30). Beginning his concluding practical exhortations (3:1), he suddenly changes the subject to a warning against the Judaizers (3:2-11) and against an antinomian teaching that since salvation is already assured there is no need of active Christian

effort or morality (3:12—4:1). After renewed concluding exhortations (4:2–9) he expresses warm-hearted
thanks for the gift received at the hand of Epaphroditus
(4:10–20) and closes with salutations and a benediction
(4:21–23).

While the letter reflects no crisis such as developed
among the Galatian churches or at Corinth, it is none
the less interesting. Because of the very fact that it is
an expression of regard sent to the most loyal of his
churches it has a richness and a beauty which throw
welcome light upon the more personal side of Paul's
character and Christian teaching.

3. LETTERS TO PHILEMON, TO THE COLOSSIANS, AND TO THE EPHESIANS

On one occasion Paul dispatched as many as three
letters together. When Philemon (especially vs. 10) is
read along with Colossians (especially 4:9) it appears at
once that both letters were sent at the same time in
company with Onesimus. Furthermore, a comparison
of Col. 4:7 with Eph. 6:21 joins these two letters
together, because Tychicus is mentioned as accompanying each; and this indication is borne out by the simi-
larity of the two in content and in the situations
portrayed both of writer and readers.

All three letters mention Paul's bonds (Philem. 1, 13;
Col. 4:18; Eph. 3:1; 4:1). While it is possible that in
case Paul was imprisoned in Ephesus these letters as
well as Philippians may have been written from that
city, the almost universal opinion of scholars points to
the Roman imprisonment as the time and place of
writing.

1. The letter to Philemon was a purely personal note. Philemon was a resident of Colossae, evidently a man of some ability and influence, for he not only owned slaves but had offered his home as a meeting-place for the church at Colossae. Onesimus, one of his slaves, had run away. Paul was sending him back. The name Onesimus means "a profitable one." In his note Paul questions whether this runaway slave was really "a profitable one" (vs. 11).

Paul returned the slave as a converted man, who had once more become a "profitable" servant, promising to pay Philemon whatever had been stolen. When Philemon received the note and read Paul's request that he treat Onesimus "no longer as a bondservant, but . . . . a brother beloved," he no doubt hesitated somewhat at this drastic Christian teaching. But he would feel the honor of receiving a note from Paul written with his "own hand" (vs. 19) and would be gratified at the hope which Paul held out of a personal visit in the no distant future (vs. 22).

2. Philemon's house at Colossae was used as a meeting-place for a Christian church (Philem., vs. 2). When Paul sent the personal note he accompanied it with a letter to be read to the church and to all Christians at Colossae. Paul had heard of teachings which were confusing and unsettling them in their faith. Because of the seriousness of the situation Paul sent also a personal representative and fellow-worker, Tychicus (Col. 4:7). The probable source of Paul's information was Epaphras, himself a Colossian, who was with Paul when he wrote. Epaphras had been a "fellow-servant" with Paul probably at Ephesus and had

subsequently preached to the Colossians (1:6, 7). While writing, Paul may have asked him frequent questions in order to obtain accurate information for use in his letter.

The teachings which were perverting the gospel in Colossae were not unrelated to the geographical location of the city in the interior of the province of Asia on the highway between eastern and western civilization and thought. They were related in general to the mystery-religions, and in particular to the mystic communion with heavenly powers, which was a fundamental doctrine of those cults. The Colossian Christians were being led into the idea that, in the quest of this mystic communion, the "fulness" of religious experience, i.e., the sense of being filled with divine power, was to be found in communion, not merely with Christ, but with other heavenly powers as great as, perhaps greater than, Christ.

Along with the teaching of mystic communion were associated certain ascetic practices. "Handle not, nor taste, nor touch" are "ordinances" which had their place in the preparatory rites of the mystery-religions as described in chapter i of this volume. The situation was further complicated by the presence of Judaizing tendencies, some of which may have been connected with the ascetic teachings. Circumcision, observance of Jewish Sabbaths, of new moons, of Jewish feasts, of seasons of fasting, all find reference in the epistle.

Paul's plan of procedure was not to attack all these ideas as worthless and as opposed to Christian faith. He adopted the attitude of conciliation. From their point of view and, so far as possible, in their language and thought world, he interpreted to the Colossians the supreme greatness of Christ. Through all the centuries Christianity has come in contact with other thought movements, both philosophical and religious, and has come to terms with them, not by simply rejecting or accepting, but by careful selection and interpretation and adjustment.

Using their vocabulary Paul tells the Colossians that in Christ "dwelleth all the fulness of the godhead bodily." In regard to circumcision he declares that in Christ they "were also circumcised with a circumcision not made with hands." In regard to the attractive symbolic lustrations of the mystery-religions (see chapter i of this volume) he explains that in Christian baptism they were buried with Christ and raised with him through faith. Observances of feasts and new moons are a shadow of Christian truth. In Christ everything and every people find completion and unity. This is the perfect "mystery." In Christ "are all the treasures of wisdom." The Greek has his "philosophy" and the Jew "circumcision"; but in Christ "there cannot be Greek and Jew, circumcision and uncircumcision, Barbarian, Scythian, bondman, freeman; but Christ is all and in all."

In writing the letter Paul begins after the salutation (Col. 1:1, 2) to win his readers by personal words of thanks (1:3-8) and of prayer for their fuller understanding of Christ's supreme place (1:9-23), and by recounting his own sufferings for the gospel (1:24-29) and his particular concern for their welfare (2:1-7). He then gives his central message, a warning against philosophical teachings and Judaizing tendencies which would

rob them of the highest Christian faith (2:8–23). He
applies his message in practical exhortations to live the
higher life in the various phases of their daily conduct
(3:1—4:6). His concluding page is full of interesting
personal references to his fellow-workers (4:7–18).

Tychicus (4:7) is the bearer of this letter and of
Ephesians (6:21). The description of Onesimus (4:9)
as "one of you" establishes the fact that Philemon, his
master, lived at Colossae and incidentally suggests the
possibility that Onesimus as servant in the house where
the Christians met may have overheard such phrases
as "freedom from bondage" and "redeemed by Christ."
In his simplicity of mind he may have been led to
think that Paul, the great apostle of Christ, could somehow liberate him from slavery. Aristarchus, Mark,
Epaphras, Luke are all familiar to us (cf. also Philem.,
vs. 23, 24). Archippus (4:17; cf. Philem., vs. 2) was evidently the leader of the church in Philemon's home and
may have been Philemon's son.

Of especial interest is Paul's word, Col. 4:16, "When
this epistle hath been read among you, cause that it be
read also in the church of the Laodiceans; and that ye
also read the epistle from Laodicea." Colossae was
about six miles away. It was not unnatural that Paul
should write two similar letters to these two places at
the same time. But what has become of the letter to
the Laodiceans?

3. In Ephesians the first fact which strikes the attention of the reader is that the phrase "at Ephesus" is
uncertain. It is not found in the two oldest manu-
scripts. Moreover, although Paul spent longer in
Ephesus than anywhere else, this letter is quite imper-

sonal and distant in tone. Some expressions seem to imply that he was writing to strangers whom he had never seen. For example, he speaks in Eph. 1:15 in a very distant way of "having heard of the faith in the Lord Jesus which is among you" (cf. also 3:2). It is quite possible that this letter is the one mentioned in Col. 4:16 as the Laodicean letter. Marcion in the second century had a letter of Paul "to the Laodiceans" in his canon, which apparently was in the place of our Ephesians. Origen mentions it also.

It is not hard to understand how the name Ephesians came to be attached to a letter sent to Laodicea. Perhaps Paul wished it sent, not only from Laodicea to Colossae, as he requested in Col. 4:16, but also to other churches in Asia. Its impersonal character accords well with the idea that it was a circular epistle. In this case it would naturally come at length to Ephesus, the capital, and be kept there. A later collector finding it there might conclude it was written to the Ephesians, or at least might consider that if it was meant for several churches it had a right to be called by the name of the chief church in Asia.

The letter is somewhat similar to Colossians in general structure and almost identical in many of its exhortations (cf. especially Eph. 5:22—6:9 with Col. 3:18—4:1). After the expression of praise and thanksgiving (chap. 1) he contrasts their earlier un-Christian state with the present building up of all believers into one great temple, one body in Christ (chap. 2). Then he describes the "mystery" of Christ and prays that in him they may find the "fulness" of God which they seek (chap. 3). He exhorts them to leave their old manner of life with its various evils (chap. 4) and to live in a sober Christian way each in his own place (chaps. 5, 6).

The fact that Ephesians is in many ways so similar to the letter to Colossae has led many to doubt its genuineness, and to suppose that some later writer familiar with Asia Minor's philosophical and religious teachings composed the letter, using Colossians as a model. But there is really no reason why Paul should not have sent two similar letters at the same time to neighboring churches. There are some scholars who question whether both letters are not quite foreign to Paul's style. It is true that a vocabulary is here used which is not found elsewhere in Paul. But the ideas and contentions are genuinely Pauline, and it is not at all impossible to believe that Paul could thus express himself in the language and thought world of those whom he wished to win.

Ephesians has a broader point of view than Colossians. The Colossian perversion of the gospel serves in Ephesians only as a point of departure for a general warning against any teaching which does not recognize the supreme majesty of Christ. Controversies and false doctrines are almost forgotten as Paul unfolds the eternal plan of God through all the ages to consummate all things in Christ. That all men may have "the unsearchable riches of Christ," may "know the love of Christ which passeth knowledge," "may be filled unto all the fulness of God"—this is Paul's prayer. The great international company of believers is the body of Christ, through whom God has from all eternity purposed to reveal his glorious salvation.

4. THE END OF THE FIGHT

Did Paul ever realize his project of a trip to Spain (Rom. 15:24)? We have no account of the journey nor of any further experiences after the two years in Rome. Many scholars conclude from the ominous silence of Acts that Paul did not survive his imprisonment. We ought not, however, to accept this conclusion without noting some of the facts which point to a further career of activity.

1. The lively hope which Paul expresses in Rom., chap. 15, would not by itself constitute any argument. But in the repeated representations of the Book of Acts that Paul was treated with a considerable degree of justice by the Roman authorities we are rather definitely led to expect that he was able to carry out his proposed journey.

2. Clement of Rome, who wrote an epistle to the Corinthian church before the close of the first century, speaks in no uncertain terms of Paul as "having taught righteousness unto the whole world and having reached the farthest bounds of the West." Clement must have himself been able to remember Paul's closing years, or at least to have talked with those who had known Paul. To say that Clement's phrase, "farthest bounds of the West"[1] (Clement, I Cor., chap. 5), means the center of the world, where Clement lived and wrote, sounds like juggling with words.

3. In Acts 1:1 Luke refers to his gospel as the "first" (not *former*) treatise, suggesting, although not necessarily implying, that he intended to write at least three

[1] τὸ τέρμα τῆς δύσεως.

books. This third work of Luke has been the subject of much speculation. It would account for the abrupt ending of the Book of Acts. It would accord in general with the statement of Eusebius that Paul died in the thirteenth year of Nero, and also with his other statement that Paul died in the Neronian persecution.

4. The argument from the Pastoral Epistles has little weight because scholars have doubted their genuineness in whole or in part. But in any case they add their evidence such as it is; for a later writer composing these epistles would not inject them into a situation of the apostle which he believed never existed. They at least reflect an early Christian tradition that Paul was released from the first Roman imprisonment (cf. especially II Tim. 4:16, 17).

5. Finally the Muratorian Canon adds its evidence. This is a list of New Testament books compiled in the latter part of the second century. In commenting on the Book of Acts this canon remarks on the fact that the book does not record the death of Peter and the journey of Paul from Rome to Spain. There can be little doubt that the author regarded Paul's journey to Spain as a historical fact.

If Luke did write a third book—and it is not impossible to understand the Muratorian Canon as referring to this third work—he perhaps, on the analogy of Acts, devoted the first half of it to the further experiences of Jewish Christian leaders, including the martyrdom of Peter, and the second half to further journeys of Paul and to his martyrdom.

On the supposition that the Pastoral Epistles are genuine the usual reconstruction of these later journeys of Paul is somewhat as follows: Paul is acquitted at Rome perhaps on condition that he remain an exile from Judea. He embarks for Spain. He spends some time planting the gospel along the coast. He then returns to visit his earlier churches. He pays the promised visit to Philemon. He leaves Timothy in charge at Ephesus. Visits Macedonia. Writes I Timothy. Leaves Macedonia to preach in Crete, stopping at Troas and Miletus on the way. He plants the gospel in Crete. Leaving Titus in charge there he revisits Corinth, where he writes a letter to Titus. From Corinth he makes a tour overland northward to Nicopolis, where his enemies finally secure his arrest. He is taken to Rome, where he writes II Timothy shortly before his death.

But the lack of direct information and the questioning of the genuineness of at least parts of the Pastoral Epistles are serious objections to any assertion of probability in such a reconstruction. Its chief support is in the statement of Clement of Rome mentioned above.

In regard to the place and approximate date of the apostle's death there is, however, no real question. That he died in Rome and during the reign of Nero, probably not long after 61 A.D., we may regard as practically certain. Clement of Rome and Caius of Rome both speak of his martyrdom there. Both Origen and Eusebius place his death at Rome and under Nero. Eusebius says that he was beheaded.

That "his eye was not dim nor his natural force abated" we may be sure. The words of II Tim. 4:7, 8 are an expression of the spirit which we may be sure he maintained to the very end: "I have fought the good fight, I have finished the course, I have kept the faith: henceforth there is laid up for me the crown of righteousness, which the Lord, the righteous judge, shall give to me at that day; and not to me only, but also to all them that have loved his appearing."

5. PAUL'S PLACE IN CHRISTIANITY

At Paul's conversion Christianity was a Jewish sect. At his death it was a world-religion. While there were others who carried the gospel among the nations, their work is almost lost to sight beside the brighter glory of Paul's achievement. Somewhat as America has enlarged her hope of a great ideal commonwealth and has realized her place among the nations, so through Paul's powerful leadership the early Christian movement developed into an international brotherhood. He led the Christian religion far toward the day when it was officially recognized as the supreme religion of the empire.

His power lay partly in the message with which he started and partly in the breadth and strength of personality with which he interpreted and universalized his message.

The background or basis of his message was the Jewish religion of the Old Testament. Paul taught the doctrine of one God, the Father. His positive affirmation that there is but one God was in sharp contrast to the hesitating and philosophical monotheism of Stoicism, the equally hesitant polytheism of Epicureanism, the decadent polytheism of the state religions, and the inclusive pantheon of the mystery-religions. For Paul all these and the older henotheism of the Jews were left behind, their place being taken by *one* God, who made heaven and earth and directs all human affairs (I Thess. 1:9, 10; I Cor. 8:6, etc.). His passionate monotheism was a flame as intense as that in which the sarcasm of Isaiah (40:18 ff.; 44:12–20) burns up idolatrous worship.

This Jewish monotheism Paul made alive through his Christian affirmation of the one Revealer of God, Jesus, the risen Son of God, the Christ. Originally the conception of messiahship was Jewish. But Paul interpreted and enlarged its significance. In Greek language and thought forms he pictured the Crucified, the Revealer of God's love, risen to the right hand of God, acting as mediator between God and man, dwelling through his spirit in men and raising them with him into a divine life with God. This was the way of salvation for which men and women were looking. Through Paul's preaching they were able to lay hold upon Christ, to rise into a newness of life, and to look eagerly for a future fuller revelation of God in human affairs.

The real key which unlocked the gates of the early Christian tide of evangelism was Paul's powerful and practical universalism. His love of totality made henotheism monotheism, made God's love for Israel a love for a spiritual Israel composed of people of every nation. He declared that religion is not a matter of ceremonial or legalistic observances. Over against the Jewish legal system he stood for a religion of the spirit. Even baptism and the Lord's supper and Christian observances were not ceremonies which procured merit before God but helps to entering into fellowship with Christ and being filled with his spirit. This spirit was the controlling power in his life. In place of a

Jewish legalistic commonwealth he founded the spiritual democracy of self-legislating love.

In proclaiming the messianic kingdom so familiar to the synagogue worshipers, the distinctive note which he introduced along with the messiahship of Jesus was the broader, international aspect of the coming order. He did not paint the Jews as sole possessors of divine revelation sitting on twelve thrones judging the nations of the world. Circumcision and uncircumcision were alike without religious significance. The Greek was brother of the "Barbarian." In the Roman Empire the association of various nationalities was such as has perhaps never been paralleled until our own day in America. Greeks, Barbarians, Scythians, Jews, Romans, all, he declared, were alike in Christ, whether bond or free, man or woman.

The Jewish church, accepting Jesus as the Messiah, but confining his salvation within narrow legalistic limits, could make no large appeal, could win no large following. Paul, discovering in faith in Jesus as the Son and Revealer of God and in fellowship with him a way of righteousness that made subjection to legal statutes superfluous and impertinent, opened the door of hope to all nations. With him Christianity became in hope and potentiality a world-religion. Jewish Christianity dwindled and perished. Pauline Christianity conquered, and is still conquering, the world.

The mystery-religions perished. Paul's mystery-religion, if such it may be called, triumphed. It was again his freedom from local and national rites and ceremonies, his insistence upon a monotheistic spiritual and universal worship, and the vividness and intensity of his broad democratic conception of the international brotherhood in the "Kingdom" which outstripped those other religions.

This love of totality breathed through his entire missionary planning. He saw before his mind the provinces of the Roman Empire and aimed to have Christ preached to them all. He could not speak of a man as his first convert in Ephesus but as "the first-fruits of Asia." If a man was converted in Athens, the name of that city is not mentioned; he was "the first-fruits of Achaia." Distant Spain was not forgotten.

The universalism of Jesus was intensive. The universalism of Paul was extensive. Jesus showed that he loved the world by showing his love for its dregs, whether publican or harlot, and for outsiders, whether for Syro-Phoenician woman or Roman centurion. The universalism of Jesus cannot be exaggerated. But the actual realization of it was left to the apostle. Paul died before he had covered the geographic area of the Roman Empire, but his immortal travels easily reveal the totality of his purpose.

Geography and astronomic space and ages of history seem to mingle together in his far-traveled spirit. All the psychologic categories are in him. Space is there with its height and depth. Time is there with its things present and things to come. All possible conditions are there between the extremes of life and death, and phantasmal beings real and unreal, whether angels or principalities or powers, and even any other new creation as yet unknown (Rom. 8:38, 39).

And this is the true view for practical religion of the much-discussed relation between Paul and Jesus. He who would have the universal gospel in his soul must have Jesus with him in the still air of his studies. He must live in his closet and in his place of retreat with the Jesus of the gospels. But as he starts out for missionary service, as he betakes himself to sociological study or sociological toil, as he reaches out toward the blessed democracy of the realized Kingdom of God among men, as he aims to combine patriotism with the love of mankind, let him take with him the citizen of no mean city, who made of the simple Jewish gospel concerning the Christ an instrument for the bringing of salvation to men of every nation, the man who was a debtor to Greek and to Barbarian so long as any land was unvisited by his missionary toil, the man who must see Rome also. Let him take with him Paul.

SUPPLEMENTARY READING

1. Foakes-Jackson, *Saint Paul*, pp. 221–40.
2. McNeile, A. H., *St. Paul*, pp. 118–20; 203–64.
3. Wood, C. T., *Life of Paul*, pp. 308–87.
4. Ramsay, *St. Paul the Traveller*, pp. 344–62.
5. Kent, *Work and Teachings of the Apostles*, pp. 220–23; 231–37.
6. Gilbert, *Student's Life of Paul*, pp. 216–32.
7. Conybeare and Howson, *Life and Epistles of St. Paul*, chaps. xxiv–xxvii.
8. Farrar, *Life and Work of St. Paul*, chap. lvii.
9. *Bible for Home and School*, "Acts," pp. 253–58.
10. McGiffert, *A History of Christianity in the Apostolic Age*, pp. 362–423.
11. Cone, *Paul the Man, the Missionary, and the Teacher*, pp. 144–45.
12. Bacon, *The Story of St. Paul*, pp. 214–26; 298–380.

CHAPTER XIII

PAUL'S RELIGION

1. GENERAL CHARACTER OF HIS MESSAGE

What was it which so gripped and held Paul's listeners in every city to which he came? What was that message which, transmitted through Paul's simple words, "turned the world upside down"? What made the fortune-teller of Philippi give up her business? What made the ship-loader at Corinth rise an hour earlier to attend the Christian meeting? What made the men of Troas listen eagerly while Paul discoursed past midnight? What made those busy Christians of Rome come forty miles on the way to meet Paul?

We can be very sure that Paul's message was something that affected vitally the daily life of those who listened to it; that Paul showed men a way of definitely knowing and feeling the presence of God in their lives, a way of making their days count for eternity. Paul turned men's thoughts away from themselves to a world waiting for redemption, he gave them a picture of God large enough not only to solve their personal problems but to include all classes of men and especially such ones as those men of Macedonia who contributed out of their "deep poverty" (II Cor. 8:2).

The heart of Paul's religion was his loyalty to Jesus Christ. He felt that the spirit of Jesus was the greatest uplifting power in the world, able to raise any man or woman above the difficulties and baseness of life into an exalted walk with God. "I determined not to know anything among you save Jesus Christ and him crucified" (I Cor. 2:2). Jesus had brought into the world a great new sacrificial idealism which he had lived and taught even to the giving up of his own life. But the work of Jesus was not finished. Paul "carried on," and in his own person was "making up for what was lacking in the sufferings of Jesus" (Col. 1:24). Paul put Jesus into the hot spot of his consciousness and became a "new creature" (Gal. 6:15; II Cor. 5:17) in a realm of service and fellowship and world-brotherhood.

2. THE LETTERS

In a reconstruction of Paul's way of approaching men and women, our primary source of information is the collection of his letters. Recent years of research have thrown much new light upon the character and spirit of these writings. In the Roman Empire at large, the century from Caesar to Nero was a century of extraordinary literary activity. To this period belong the names of Caesar, Cicero, Sallust, Horace, Vergil, Livy, Strabo, Ovid, Seneca, Philo, Josephus, and a host of others. In striking contrast to the multiplying of literary production, and especially in contrast to the increased reverence of the Jews for their book of Scriptures, Paul traveled through the cities of the Empire without any book of Christian teaching. His Christianity was not a book religion. He felt that the spirit of Jesus in his heart was the best authority for Christian conduct and worship. His religion was a religion of life, a religion of a quickening, pulsating spirit which unites men to God.

There are two kinds of epistles. We might distinguish the two kinds by calling one "epistle" and the other "letter." Jesus did not, like Mohammed, write a Koran. Neither did Paul write epistles in the sense in which we speak of the "epistles of Horace." Paul was no mere analytical philosopher, nor was he absorbed in the beauty of eloquent oratory like Apollos. He was one who taught by his life.

He lived in the lives of his Christian converts. He worked with them in their weaving. He was glad when they were glad, he suffered when they suffered. He knew what it was to be hungry, to be wounded, to be shipwrecked both by land and by sea. His life was lost in the life of his Christian brothers. And he meant it to be so. "You are our epistle, known and read of all men, written not with ink but with the spirit of the living God" (II Cor. 3:2).

An epistle of Horace or an epistle of Jeremiah was meant for publication and for general information, or edification. The letters of Paul expressed gratitude for particular acts or gifts, affection for certain people, warnings based upon experience with local influences or evils. An epistle is a piece of art; a letter is a piece of life. The difference is as great as the difference between a dialogue of Plato and a conversation which you and I hold on the street corner. One is like the carefully finished photograph which "does you justice"; the other is like a snapshot which shows you as you are.

The letters of Paul are genuine letters. As such, they are perhaps more precious than more formal epistles would be. In them we see not only Paul's thoughts and opinions, but we see Paul himself in all his greatness and intensity, not dead but alive; a man whose spirit is so eternal that he can be all things to all men. As we read his letters we can hear him calling insistently through the megaphone of the centuries, "I am not a book; I am a man." He who truly reads his letters sees not the pages and the ink but looks through them as through a window clear as crystal into the house and home of Paul's soul and into that glowing fire which sheds its radiance into "the farthest bounds of the West."

Each letter has its particular message or messages.

1. In writing to Philemon, Paul is sorry for the runaway slave and wishes to make easier the servant's resolve to return to his master. To understand the letter as a treatise embodying the Christian teaching that runaway slaves should always be sent back to their masters is to pervert Paul's attitude. The little note is rather a personal plea to Philemon to recognize that in the Christian life a slave is to be treated as a brother and fellow-man, not as an animal.

2. In the Thessalonian letters, Paul's message is again to definite individuals, exhorting them to quickened hope and to renewed patience in living worthily of their calling.

3. In Galatians he is fighting certain ones who tried

to undermine his gospel by teaching that Christians must keep a code of laws and observances. To his Galatian friends, he emphasizes the absolute freedom of the man who is filled with the spirit of Christ from all statutory regulations.

4. In writing to the Corinthians, he opposes their inclinations to form factions in accordance with their various ways of stating the gospel. In opposition to their Greek love for theory and disregard of practice, Paul emphasizes the essentials of Christian conduct. His message to them is that the Christian spirit, far from being a spirit of philosophic wrangling, is a spirit of love which begins with the self-sacrifice of the cross and rises to the gifts of the spirit (chaps. 12–14); "and the greatest of these is love" (13:13).

5. Romans is the most impersonal of the letters because Paul had not been in Rome. He explains the relation of his gospel to non-Christian and especially Jewish systems of salvation. He shows how helpless they have been to lead men into the higher life. But even in Romans we hear the echo of his own personal experience. Paul had himself experienced the power of Christ to raise men who were dead in trespass and sin. "Sin revived and I died . . . . Wretched man that I am! who shall deliver me out of the body of this death? I thank God through Jesus Christ our Lord "(Rom. 7:25).

6. Colossians and Ephesians have their warning against theosophic teachings about angels and hierarchies of heavenly beings which separate God from man. Again Paul's emphasis is upon the full possession of the saving power that is in Christ and upon the conduct befitting those who live in him.

7. Finally, Philippians is a letter of personal thanks for the loyalty and generosity of his beloved church expressed in the gift which he had received. Paul's message is one of rejoicing in the midst of his imprisonment—such a joy as he hopes they may continually experience in their exalted Christian life.

If in these various messages we look for a common emphasis which we can call Paul's supreme message, we see in every letter the thought that through the uplifting power of the spirit of Jesus men may live on earth a life which is above earthly limitations—a kind of superlife. Distinctions between master and slave melt away (Phil.). Christian communities like the one at Thessalonica begin to realize in a small way the glory of the day when the whole earth shall belong to Christ (Thess.). Men who live the superlife are independent of all law and commandment (Gal.). They have died to flesh and common desires and have risen with Christ into the marvelous life of the spirit by virtue of which they bear now the fruits of the spirit and at the coming of the Lord are glorified with him (Cor.). Roman and Greek and Jewish ways of attaining eternal life have faded away (Rom.). Theosophic systems have become useless (Col., Eph.). The joy of the new superlife is irresistible and unquenchable (Phil.).

3. THE NEW POWER AND THE NEW LIFE

Paul had discovered a new power. His discovery was more revolutionary than the discovery of electricity, or gas engine, or wireless. As electricity has been applied to the needs of civilization, so Paul went about explaining and applying his new discovery. The difference is that

Paul's discovery was inestimably more important—a discovery of the way by which the soul of man may attain eternal health and life.

Paul had personally experienced the power. His own life had been completely changed. Instead of a bondage of law and sin, he had through the new power attained freedom, and a joyous life. He had discovered the greatest thing in the world and in the universe and in eternity.

Jesus had revealed it to him. Jesus triumphed over evil and suffering and death. Paul had received the power of the living Christ into his soul, and had attained fellowship and union with God. He was a new creature. He no longer lived an earthly existence but a heavenly one, hand in hand with Christ.

He told men that he no longer lived in the flesh, but in the spirit. Flesh is mortal and corruptible. No man need any longer live in the flesh, governed by bodily desires and selfish comforts. If the spirit of Christ enters into a man and he lives in that spirit, he rises above all these material things. The way to attain the higher life is by close union with Christ. If we suffer with him (Rom. 8:17), if we are crucified with him (Gal. 2:20), if we die with him (Rom. 6:8), if we are buried with him (Col. 2:12), then we are raised with him (Rom. 6:4) and live with him (Rom. 6:8).

Christ was the first progenitor of a new race. Just as Adam was our father according to the flesh, so Jesus was our first Father according to the spirit. He sowed the seed of the higher life in the souls of his apostles, and they have given of that life to their spiritual children throughout the world. Men are as truly born a second time, born of the spirit, as they are born once of the flesh. The new race and the new family are as much more glorious than the old as the Garden of Eden was more beautiful than the primeval chaos over which the spirit of God brooded (II Cor. 4:6). Christ was the second Adam (I Cor. 15:45; Rom. 5:12, 17). Any man who lives in Christ is a new creature living in a newly created spiritual Garden of Eden. Old things have passed away. All things have become new.

Many marvelously rich words Paul used in the expressing of this new divine experience. Some have a double and triple content. The "love of Christ" (II Cor. 5:14) means not merely our love for Christ nor even Christ's love for us. It signifies primarily the Christlike love which we have in us toward our fellowmen. The "hope of Christ" (I Thess. 1:3) is not merely a hope of Christ's coming, nor Christ's hope for us, but is that glorious optimism which fills our souls in Christ. The peace of Christ, the gentleness of Christ, the patience of Christ are all notes in the harmony of the soul which knows him in the new mystic life of the Spirit. Men felt themselves enriched with the "riches of Christ." In this superearthly existence they received a power like the "power of Christ" so that they could "do all things."

The relation between this divine indwelling spirit and Christ is very close. To be sure Paul thinks of Christ as the Jewish Messiah exalted to heaven and standing at the right hand of God, just as Stephen had seen him when Paul was standing by. On the other hand, in the language of Socrates and of Greek thought and of the mystery-religions, he speaks of the heavenly spirit dwelling in his own soul. Concerning this heavenly spirit he uses the same phrases which he employs of Christ. In one passage he speaks of being in Christ (I Cor. 1:30). In another passage he speaks of being in the spirit (Rom. 8:9). In Phil. 4:1, he exhorts to stand fast in Christ. In Phil. 1:27, he exhorts to stand fast in one spirit. In II Cor. 2:17, we speak in Christ. In I Cor. 12:3 we speak in the spirit. In Rom. 12:15, we are one body in Christ. In I Cor. 12:13, we are one body in the spirit. The list is almost endless. Faith, righteousness, justification, sanctification, grace, love, peace are all at one time "in Christ," and at another time "in the spirit." Rejoicing, bearing witness, circumcision, being filled, making intercession are all "in Christ" and also in the spirit. We are God's temple in Christ and in the spirit. Christ dwells in the believer and so does the spirit.

This spirit, so closely related to Christ, was an inner power sending men out in search of others, directing men's thoughts upward to God as to a beneficent father, urging men to their highest capacity of living the life of God as revealed in Christ. The manifestations of the power of the spirit were to Paul an "earnest"-money, a "first instalment" of the promised new humanity of the future.

The Apostolic conference[1] gave Paul new courage to preach his idea of salvation. He went forth again, more determined than ever before, to tell the Jews of the Dispersion "that a man is not justified by the works of the Law" in any manner whatsoever (Gal. 2:16).

He tells the Galatians that the Law was only temporary, that even Abraham, the patron saint of Judaism, had no Law. He argued from the Old Testament itself,

[1] See pp. 93-110.

that "the righteous shall live by faith" (Gal. 3:11, quoted from Hab. 2:4); and "the Law is not of faith" (Gal. 3:12). He uses many other arguments which it is not our place here to review.

As Paul was welcomed by great numbers of the Jews of the Dispersion, he told how he, himself, had been freed from the oppression of the old religion. He was a living example of the optimism and buoyancy and fulness of life which he preached. Jews everywhere were caught by the contagion of it. They were filled with his spirit and the spirit of Jesus.

The new attitude became so plainly superior to the old that Paul at one time had to answer the question whether non-Christian Jews will be saved at all (Rom. 9–11). It was a difficult question, and Paul wrestled with it until his heart was sore within him. His answer was that God, in his own way, somehow, sometime, will also save his chosen people as he was saving the Gentiles. It was an indefinite but a truly Christian answer.

One of the best ways of describing Paul's religion, as distinguished from the Jewish, is to say that Judaism was a negative religion, as compared with the positive freedom and activity of Paul's Christian spirit. Nowhere in Scripture is this so beautifully depicted as in Galatians, chapter 5: "Walk by the Spirit," says Paul, "and you will not fulfill the lust of the Flesh." It is Paul's way of saying that we can graduate from the petty, physical passions and the laws regarding physical matters, by rising into the higher realm of a spiritual walk with God. Instead of avoiding what is degrading, we should reach out after what is uplifting. Instead of repeating the Decalogue each morning after breakfast, or wearing a scroll of the prohibitions upon our foreheads, as some of the old rabbis did, we should do as the modern Boy Scouts do—we should resolve each day to do some positive service to someone. Shall we keep our minds upon the terrible and fearful list of things to be avoided, as given in Gal. 5:19–21, or shall we turn to the list of the fruits of the spirit, where "there is no law" (Gal 5:22, 23)?

4. GREEK PHILOSOPHY AND THE MYSTERY-RELIGIONS

The fundamental teaching of Stoicism was allied to the philosophy of Plato. Plato found a dualism in human life. There is the material, the physical, the transitory, the imperfect; and over against this is the ideal toward which men strive, the spiritual, the immaterial, the eternal. The Stoics held that God is an immaterial and invisible spirit, guiding all things. A man's soul is akin to the spiritual. In fact, Epictetus, perhaps the greatest of the Stoics, is famous for his statement that we are all of us "fragments of God," because each one of us has a spiritual nature or soul, a spark of the divine. The Stoics thought of all good men as sons of God. This philosophy raised men above the temptations and trials of the flesh. It exalted human life and enabled men to live a superphysical existence. This Stoic way of life was, in many respects, not far from the Christian way.

The Stoic philosophy made possible a much higher type of religion than had existed in the preceding centuries. To be sure, people in Ephesus still cried, on occasion, "Great is Diana of the Ephesians" (Acts 19:28). But there were also other religions more in line with the enlightened life of the day. One of these religions is known as the "Eleusinian Mysteries." This was really the national religion of the Greeks.

In the far-distant past, it was founded upon the story of Persephone. Every book of Greek mythology has this story. The beautiful young maiden, daughter of Demeter, was picking flowers one day, when she was snatched away by Aides, or Pluto, the god of the underworld, the world of the dead. When her mother, Demeter (symbolic of Mother Earth) discovered the theft, she was inconsolable. She wept and mourned until a compromise was arranged, by which Pluto, the god of the dead, gave back the girl to her mother for six months, on condition that, at the end of six months, he might have her again for another six months. The legend, of course, is the story of the alternation of winter and summer. Mother Earth rejoices in the spring, as over the return of a long-lost daughter. She mourns and weeps when fertility and life have been snatched away to the realms of the dead.

This story became the foundation of a religion of a very wide appeal. Anyone who has read the modern novel *If Winter Comes* easily understands the teaching of this religion. It was this: As truly as Persephone came back from the realm of the dead, as truly as winter yields to spring and summer, so truly may a man, though he be dead, yet live again. This teaching was applied in a double way. There was the assurance that, at the end of life, there comes a resurrection in the life hereafter; and there was also the present experience that the sorrows of life cannot overwhelm, but can give way to brighter days and to the victory of the spirit.

The relation of all this to Stoicism is plain and simple. Stoicism taught the presence of an indwelling Spirit, uplifting and exalting. The Eleusinian mysteries gave the invitation to any man: Join the great religion which is as true and unquestionable as the alternation of the winter and summer. When you join and share in the sacraments and rituals, a new supply and fulness of divine spirit will exalt you above your old life, as far as the springtime is above the coldness and darkness of winter. As surely as Persephone came back from the dead, so surely shall you be freed from darkness and death, and transported into a springtime of life and fruitfulness.

There were other religions, such as "the Mysteries of Attis," which were very similar. There was a bad side to some of these religions. But the superiority of the Christian religion has become so plainly established in modern times that it is no longer necessary to hunt for evil things to say about non-Christian religions. We can afford to look on the good side.

Anyone taking this sympathetic attitude toward the religions which Paul met will find the pages of his letters full of meanings which cannot otherwise be understood. Paul taught that the spirit of God may dwell in us bringing life out of death and beauty out of darkness. When Paul preached the resurrection of Jesus to the Greeks, it came to them as a very natural idea and had for them at first this very simple meaning. As surely as Jesus triumphed over death (i.e., as surely as spring follows winter), so surely in the soul of any man or woman may a winter of cheerlessness give way to a summer of fruitfulness.

5. JUSTIFICATION BY FAITH

On the old basis, a Jew kept the Law with the idea that a day of reckoning will come at the inauguration of the

Messianic Kingdom. Every Jew will appear before the Judgment Seat. If his record is right, he will be pronounced "justified" and will enter into his reward. This is what is known as the "forensic" sense of the word "righteousness."

Paul's own idea is that religion has its chief value in the present rather than the future. He does not give up the future idea, but he throws all his emphasis into the present. He himself had been saved from a "wretched" existence which he calls "a living death" (Rom. 7:9, 10, 24). This "being saved" is, for him, salvation.

The word "righteousness" and its derivatives very fortunately and happily, in Greek literature had a double meaning and a double usage. That is the reason Paul is so fond of the words. "Justification" and "justify" are derived from the same root in Greek as the word used in Rom. 3:21 and elsewhere translated "righteousness."[1] The word "righteousness" was usually used by Plato and other leaders of Greek philosophy in the sense of moral uprightness of character.

Paul's idea of "righteousness" is "dynamic" and moral, rather than "forensic." This is the contribution which Paul made to those to whom he preached. They began to think less about the future and less about a divine ledger of debit and credit. They began to think more about present state of heart, more about ennobling the soul and fitting it for the higher destiny, more about spiritual living and brotherly love.

When Paul formulated his principle convictions in

[1] "Neither the moral nor the forensic element can be lost sight of" (Burton, *International Critical Commentary on Galations*, p. 469).

regard to the new way of salvation, he made "justification by faith" the chief cornerstone. Those Jews who revered the Mosaic Law held that a man will be judged according to his works. They put little emphasis upon character and upon righteousness of the heart. Paul in his fight for the freedom of the gospel said that works of the law were of no avail in saving a man. The only function of the Mosaic Law was to show a man how sinful he naturally was. Its actual effect was to discourage men. "The letter killeth."

But the spirit giveth life. The way to receive the spirit is by faith. By *faith* Paul means not any "belief," but that loyal union with Christ which is ours when we die with him (Rom. 6:8), when we in suffering and self-sacrifice crucify the flesh with the lusts and passions thereof, when we rise with him into a new life of love. Then we receive his spirit into ourselves. *Faith* is a spiritual point of contact, a channel through which Christ's spirit flows into us and makes us like him. As in baptism we symbolize our death to self; so in partaking of the body and blood of Christ at the Lord's Supper, we symbolize the receiving of the new life which infuses our members and makes us sons of God with him. Thus we are saved by faith apart from works of law.

Salvation is real change of nature, nor mere forensic justification. To be sure, the word "justification" probably meant judicial acquittal and approval in the language of those Jews whom Paul was opposing. But "justification" by faith is used metaphorically by Paul and is not exactly parallel to justification by works. Paul's great thought is that a man is made righteous by the spirit through faith, that he is born again as a son of God.

Paul's picture of Christ was thus no narrow Jewish conception of a national Messiah fulfilling national prophecy. Christ was the one for whom the whole world had been groping and feeling. The teaching of Jesus was no mere revision of the Mosaic Law. Paul took Jesus' teaching into the language and the life of the great wide world. But more than that, he took Christ from Nazareth and from Jerusalem into the great cities of the Empire. He preached the spiritual Christ, the son of God who lives not in Jerusalem but in the souls of men of every nation. Christ, the son of God, lived in Paul and in Aquila and in Priscilla. We in sordid America can hardly realize the exaltation of this thought. We have become so accustomed to the words and phrases that we have lost the driving power of the truth that lies behind them.

Paul joined heaven and earth. The Son of God is incarnate in men. He is continuing through them the work which he began in Nazareth. Jesus lives in men and they in him. Like the air we breathe, Christ in the spirit enters into us and we live in him. As pure air gives life to the body, so the spirit is the divine breath which invigorates and immortalizes the soul. The spiritual Christ is independent of time and place. The things that are seen are temporal; but the Christ whom Paul preached is international and intercenturial, universal and eternal (Rom. 8:38, 39). Christ is both with God and in the hearts of men. Christ's spirit is as truly Christ himself as the perfume is a part of the rose. His presence among men is as real as the presence of a magnetic field surrounding an electric coil.

Paul's conception of the Christian life as a life of

perfect freedom is the most exalted interpretation of Jesus which the world has known. The Jewish idea that God keeps a record of a man's acts was extremely distasteful to Paul. God has more confidence in men than that. When the apostles heard that Paul was preaching a gospel of absolute freedom, some of them were scandalized and antagonized (Acts 15:1; Gal. 2:1-10). They said that if a man is allowed free rein, he will live a life of lust and selfishness. A man must be told that God will keep a reckoning of every act. Paul tried the daring and revolutionary experiment of telling men that character is primary, and obedience to law or commandment is secondary (Gal. 2:16). Salvation is by faith. As he watched the result of this doctrine, he had the tremendous experience of seeing that when a man fully realized his eternal destiny and his responsibility in preparing for the coming of the Kingdom of God on earth, he needed no law to frighten him away from evil. The life of the spirit frees a man from the bondage of flesh (Gal. 5:16).

Paul put a new sentence into the world's creed. The old dogma "I believe in God" he supplemented with the dogma "I believe in man, filled with the spirit of Jesus" (Gal. 5:16). This is salvation, not the doing of any acts in accordance with any schedule of duty or law, but the ennobling of the soul, through the contact with the spirit of God, in Jesus.

Luther, in inaugurating the Protestant Reformation, had a similar idea. The one throws light upon the other. In his treatise on Christian Liberty he says that no work done for a reward or to avoid punishment can be called good. In order to do really noble works, a man must

first be assured of his own salvation. Life is not a pro-
bation. The good works a man does are done out of a
good heart.

> Good works do not make a good man, but a good man does
> good works. A man is justified by faith alone and not by any works
> .... and in perfect freedom does gratuitously all that he does
> seeking nothing either of profit or of salvation. . . . . Here is the
> truly Christian life; . . . . when a man applies himself with joy
> and love and . . . . serves others voluntarily and for naught.

"The love of Christ constrains us" (II Cor. 5:14).
The Christ-love dwelling in us impels us to noble living.
Paul never ceased to urge his converts to higher Christian
effort. His argument was always this: if Christ died
for us, so ought we also to help one another. The power
of the new life, the presence of the spirit, the consciousness of the indwelling Christ were irresistible.

Lives which had been lived in dreary darkness were
flooded by the sunrise of a new day (II Cor. 4:6). The
letters of Paul are full of descriptions of the exaltation
which possessed those who began to live the new life.
It was like being born again (Gal. 4:19; Rom. 8:22;
John 3:3). It was like having the inner man renewed
day by day even when the body was growing old. It was
like having drunk an elixir of life which one could feel
infusing immortal life (II Cor. 4:16). It was like being
bathed in an antiseptic healing baptism which not only
cleansed from all sin but removed all possibility of future
festering or poisoning or decay (Rom. 6:4, 19). It was
like the flood of self-respect and new power which comes
to the young man or young woman who first awakens to
a sense of a great new affection (II Cor. 11:2; I Cor. 13).
It was like the exuberance of an emancipated slave in the

days following his redemption (I Cor. 6:20; 7:23). It was like the new life which comes to long estranged friends or long separated man and wife upon the day of reconciliation or reunion (II Cor. 5:18; Rom. 5:10, 11). It was like the joy of a man who has become involved in heavy debt and has suddenly been forgiven all (Col. 2:14; Eph. 4:32). It was like the thrill of patriotism which overwhelms the good soldier in full armor on the eve of battle (Eph. 6:13–17). It was like the feeling of a prisoner who has been acquitted in a capital charge and pronounced an innocent man (Rom. 5:1; 8:35; 3:21). It was like the gratitude and thanksgiving of a young man who has just been told of his adoption (Rom. 8:23; Gal. 4:5) into a royal family and of being made an heir to great blessings by a new will and "New Testament" (II Cor. 3:6; I Cor. 11:25).

"The fruits which the spirit of Jesus produces are: love, joy, peace, patience, kindness, generosity, faithfulness, gentleness, self-mastery" (Gal. 5:22, 23).

SUPPLEMENTARY READING

1. Deissmann, *St. Paul*, pp. 139–92.
2. Foakes, Jackson, *Saint Paul*, pp. 241–50.
3. McNeile, *St. Paul*, pp. 265–307.
4. Wood, C. T., *Life of Paul*, pp. 388–400.
5. Morgan, *Religion and Theology of Paul*, pp. 113–45.
6. Deissmann, *The Religion of Jesus and the Faith of Paul*, pp. 153–278.
7. Robinson, *Gospel of John*, pp. 188–202.
8. Burton, *Commentary on Galatians* (International Critical Commentary), pp. 460–85.
9. McGiffert, *Apostolic Age*, pp. 113–50.
10. Angus, *The Mystery Religions and Christianity*, pp. 39–75.
11. Moffatt, *Paul and Paulinism*, pp. 1–75.

APPENDIX I

CHRONOLOGICAL TABLE

Paul's Career A.D.	Roman History A.D.	
	14–37	Tiberius emperor
	26–36	Pilate procurator of Judea
29		Crucifixion of Jesus
35		Paul's conversion (Acts, chap. 9)
	37–41	Caligula emperor
38		Paul visits Jerusalem (Acts 9:26)
38–47		Paul in Syria and Cilicia
	41–54	Claudius emperor (Acts 11:28)
	44	Death of Herod Agrippa I (Acts 12:23)
46		Relief visit to Jerusalem (Acts 11:30; 12:25)
47–48		First missionary journey (Acts, chaps. 13, 14)
48		Council at Jerusalem (Gal. 2:1–10; Acts, chap. 15)
49–52		Second missionary journey (Acts 15:36—18:22)
	49	Jews expelled from Rome (Acts 18:2)
50		(Beginning of year) Paul reaches Corinth
50		Letters to Thessalonians
	51	(Summer) Gallio becomes proconsul
52		Letter to Galatians
52–56		Third missionary journey (Acts 18:23—21:15)
52–55		Three years at Ephesus
	54–68	Nero emperor
55		Letters to Corinthians
56		Epistle to Romans
56		Arrival at Jerusalem
56–58		Imprisonment at Caesarea (Acts 24:27)
	58	Felix succeeded by Festus (Acts 24:27)
59		Paul reaches Rome (Acts 28:16)

Paul's Career A.D.	Roman History A.D.	
59–61		At Rome. Phil., Philemon, Col., Eph.
	64	Neronian persecution of Christians
61 (or 64)		Paul's martyrdom
	66	Jews declare war on Rome
	70	Destruction of Jerusalem

These dates agree essentially with Hastings, *Dictionary of the Bible*, article on "Chronology" (by Turner), to which the reader is referred for a full and concise discussion.   See also, in this volume, statement of the dating of Gallio's proconsulship.

APPENDIX II

A REFERENCE LIBRARY

From the endless shelves of books upon Paul it is difficult to make a selection small enough to avoid confusion. This list includes titles of books mentioned in "Supplementary Reading," together with a few additional titles for more special study. The order of their practical usefulness in connection with each chapter is given under "Supplementary Reading."

THE LIFE OF PAUL

Bacon, B. W. *The Story of St. Paul.* 1904.

Cone, O. *Paul the Man, the Missionary, and the Teacher.* 1898.

Conybeare and Howson. *Life and Epistles of St. Paul* (many editions).

Deissmann, G. A. *St. Paul* (2d ed.). New York, 1927.

Foakes-Jackson, F. J. *Life of St. Paul, the Man and the Apostle.* New York, 1926.

Gilbert, G. H. *Student's Life of Paul.* 1899.

Glover, T. R. *Paul of Tarsus.* New York, 1925.

Goodspeed, E. J. *Paul* (78 pp.). Chicago, 1922.

Kent, C. F. *Work and Teachings of the Apostles.* 1916.

Knox, W. L. *St. Paul and the Church of Jerusalem.* New York, 1925.

McGiffert, A. C. *A History of Christianity in the Apostolic Age* (2d ed.). 1899.

McNeile, A. H. *St. Paul, His Life, Letters and Christian Doctrine.* Cambridge, 1920.

Ramsay, W. M. *St. Paul the Traveller.* 1896.

——. *The Cities of St. Paul.* London, 1907.

Weizsäcker, C. *The Apostolic Age in the Christian Church* (2d ed.). 1899.

Wood, C. T. *Life, Letters and Religion of St. Paul.* New York, 1925.

Wood, Eleanor E. *Life and Ministry of Paul the Apostle.* 1912.

Among the many Lives of Paul written in popular conversational style a recent good one is:

Henry, Lyman I. *Saul, Son of Kish.* Chicago, 1924.

For boys there is a very fine little sketch by Rufus M. Jones, *St. Paul the Hero.* Macmillan, 1917.

THE LETTERS OF PAUL

Burton, E. D. *Handbook of the Life of the Apostle Paul* (5th ed.). Chicago, 1906.

Fowler, H. T. *The History and Literature of the New Testament.* New York, 1925.

Goodspeed, E. J. *Story of the New Testament.* Chicago, 1916.

Lake, K. *Earlier Epistles of St. Paul* (2d ed.). New York, 1916.

Moffatt, J. *Introduction to the Literature of the New Testament.* New York, 1911.

For detailed study of Paul's Letters:

Bible for Home and School.

International Critical Commentary.

Westminster Commentaries.

THE BOOK OF ACTS

Blunt, A. W. F. *Acts* (Clarendon Bible). 1922.

Cadbury. *The Making of Luke—Acts.* New York, 1927.

Foakes-Jackson, F. J. and Lake, K. *Beginnings of Christianity.* Part I, "The Acts of the Apostles" (3 vols.). Macmillan, 1920–, in progress.

Gilbert, G. H. "Acts" (*Bible for Home and School*).

Rackham, R. B. *The Acts of the Apostles* (*Westminster Commentary*). 1901.

PAUL'S RELIGION

Bulcock, H. *Passing and Permanent in St. Paul.* New York, 1925.

Deissmann, A. *Religion of Jesus and the Faith of Paul.* New York, 1926.

Dodd, C. H. *Meaning of Paul for Today.* New York, 1922.

Gardner, P. *Religious Experience of St. Paul.* London, 1911.

Jefferson, C. E. *The Character of Paul.* New York, 1922.

Kennedy, H. A. A. *St. Paul and the Mystery Religions.* London, 1913.

Matheson, G. *Spiritual Development of St. Paul.* 1890.

Moffatt, J. *Paul and Paulinism.* Boston, 1910.

Morgan, W. *The Religion and Theology of Paul.* Edinburgh, 1917.

Schweitzer, A. *Paul and His Interpreters.* London, 1912.

Weinel, H. *St. Paul, the Man and his Work.* New York, 1906.

Wrede, W. *Paul.* London, 1907.

LIFE IN THE GRAECO-ROMAN WORLD

Angus, S. *Environment of Early Christianity.* New York, 1915.

———. *The Mystery-Religions and Christianity.* New York, 1925. (Contains excellent bibliography.)

Case, S. J. *Evolution of Early Christianity.* Chicago, 1914.

Clemen, C. *Primitive Christianity and Its Non-Jewish Sources.* Edinburgh, 1912.

Cumont, F. *The Oriental Religions in Roman Paganism.* Chicago, 1911.

Deissmann, A. *Light from the Ancient East.* London (2d ed.), 1911. Revised and enlarged edition, Doran, 1927.

Dill, S. *Roman Society from Nero to Marcus Aurelius.* New York, 1905.

Foakes-Jackson, F. J. and Lake, K. *Beginnings of Christianity.* Vol. I. New York, 1920.

Fowler, W. W. *The Religious Experience of the Roman People.* London, 1911.

———. *Roman Ideas of Deity.* New York, 1914.

Halliday, W. R. *The Pagan Background of Early Christianity.* Liverpool, 1925.

Hastings, J. *Dictionary of the Apostolic Church* (2 vols.). New York, 1916.

Milligan, G. *Here and There among the Papyri.* London, 1922.

Robinson, B. W. *The Gospel of John.* New York, 1925.

Standard Bible Dictionary (1 vol., rev. ed.). Edited by M. W. Jacobus. New York, 1926.

Tucker, T. G. *Life in the Roman World of Nero and St. Paul.* New York, 1910.

APPENDIX III

TOPICS FOR SPECIAL STUDY

It is recommended that in connection with each chapter a special additional subject be taken up for classroom discussion, or for a lecture, or for an assigned paper.

CHAPTER I

Papyrus letters throwing light upon the New Testament: Deissmann, *Light from the Ancient East*, chap. iii; Robinson, B. W., *Biblical World*, XLIV (1914) 403 ff.

Alternative subject, The character of the Roman emperors from Augustus to Nero: *Encyclopaedia Britannica* or any history of Rome.

CHAPTER II

Trustworthiness of the Book of Acts: Ramsay, *St. Paul the Traveller*, pp. 383–90; *Bible for Home and School*, "Acts," pp. 1–22; Kent, *Work and Teachings of the Apostles*, pp. 1–8; Cadbury, *The Making of Luke-Acts;* Foakes-Jackson and Lake, *Beginnings of Christianity*, Vol. II.

Alternative subject, Gamaliel: Hastings.

CHAPTER III

Detailed comparison of the three Acts accounts of the conversion: A study of the text of Acts, chaps. 9, 22, and 26.

Alternative subject, Chronology of life of Paul: Hastings, art. "Chronology"; Burton, *Records and Letters*, pp. 201–7; Gilbert, *Student's Life of Paul*, Appendix.

CHAPTER IV

History of Antioch and the Antioch church: Hastings, art. "Antioch."

Alternative subjects, Damascus: Hastings; Cilicia: Hastings.

Possible Ephesian authorship of the imprisonment letters: B. W. Robinson in *Journal of Biblical Literature*, XXIX (1910), 181 ff.; Hastings in *Expository Times*, XXII (January, 1911), 148 ff.; C. R. Bowen, "Are Paul's Prison Letters from Ephesus?" *American Journal of Theology* (1920), pp. 112–35; 277–87.

Alternative subject. Outline analysis of Philippians, Philemon, Colossians, Ephesians: Burton, Hastings.

G. S. Duncan

Influence of the Mystery Religions upon Paul: Guignebert, *Christianity* (Macmillan, 1927), pp. 63–107. Also Case, Angus.

Alternative subject. Comparison of Paul's religion with that of the Gospel of John: B. W. Robinson, *Gospel of John*, pp. 29–44.

APPENDIX IV

OUTLINE OF A LIFE OF PAUL

There is no better way of conserving the benefits of a study of Paul's life than by personally writing out a biography of the apostle. Use the New Testament references, the suggestions of this volume, and the results of supplementary reading.

The following chapter headings are recommended as appropriate for such a study:

I. The Jews and the Jewish Dispersion
1. History of the Jews in the two centuries before Paul
2. The extent of the Dispersion. Its liberalism
3. The "devout" Greeks

II. Religious Condition of the Roman Empire
1. General social situation
2. The mystery-religions
3. Emperor-worship

III. The Preparation of the World for Christianity
1. Politically
2. Socially
3. Religiously

IV. Paul's boyhood
1. The city of Tarsus
2. Paul's family
   a) Jewish
   b) Roman
   c) The name "Saul"
3. Schooling. Learning a trade

V. Paul's Life as a Jew
1. His first view of the Temple
2. The character of Gamaliel
3. Return to Tarsus and marriage
4. The noble side of Jewish religion

INDEXES

INDEX OF SUBJECTS

255

INDEX OF SCRIPTURE REFERENCES

Christine Jezek